THE PERFORMANCE ASSESSMENT HANDBOOK

VOLUME 2
PERFORMANCES AND EXHIBITIONS

Designs from the Field and Guidelines for the Territory Ahead

Bil Johnson

EYE ON EDUCATION
P.O. BOX 3113
PRINCETON, N.J. 08543
(609) 395-0005
(609) 395-1180 fax

Editorial and production services provided by Richard H. Adin Freelance Editorial Services, 9 Orchard Drive, Gardiner, NY 12525 (914-883-5884)

ISBN 1-883001-17-X

Library of Congress Cataloging-in-Publication Data

Johnson, Bil, 1949–
          The performance assessment handbook : designs from the field
     and guidelines for the territory ahead / Bil Johnson
               p.   cm.
     Includes bibliographical references.
     ISBN 1-883001-16-1 (v. 1). — ISBN 1-883001-17-X (v. 2)
     1. Educational tests and measurements — United States — Handbooks,
manuals, etc. 2. Portfolios in education — United States — Handbooks,
manuals, etc. 3. Competency based educational tests — United States —
Handbooks, manuals, etc. I. Title.
LB3051.J566 1996
371.2'6 — dc20   95-39968
                                                                         CIP

10 9 8 7 6 5 4 3 2

If you like this book, we recommend:

THE PERFORMANCE ASSESSMENT HANDBOOK
VOLUME 1: PORTFOLIOS AND SOCRATIC SEMINARS
Designs from the Field and Guidelines for the Territory Ahead
by Bil Johnson

Dedication

To my mother, for her energy and intellect;
To my father, who taught me about teaching;
To my brother, who taught me about learning.

ABOUT THE AUTHOR

Bil Johnson is a member of the National Re: Learning Faculty of the Annenberg Institute for School Reform. He has taught secondary English and Social Studies in the public schools since 1971. Johnson has been an active member of the Coalition of Essential Schools for 10 years, and is currently Lead Teacher at the Francis W. Parker Charter School in Fort Devens, Massachusetts.

TABLE OF CONTENTS

ABOUT THE AUTHOR ix
ACKNOWLEDGMENTS xiii
AUTHOR'S NOTE xv
FOREWORD xvii
INTRODUCTION xix

1   "IS THIS GOING TO BE ON THE TEST?" TRADITIONAL
    TESTS AND PERFORMANCE ASSESSMENTS: THE
    TERRITORY AHEAD 1
    The Context of Today's Testing: Where Did
       It Come From? 2
    Testing the Tests 7
       Planning Backwards from Outcomes for
          Continuous Progress 8
       Essential Questions and Performance Assessments . 11
          A Different Approach 12
       Designing Assessments Which Embody the
          Outcomes 14
    The Larger Context 23
       Checkpoints and Mileposts 23
       You Can't Do That in My (Math, Science, Health,
          etc.) Course 25
       Performance Assessments and the Territory
          Ahead 26

2   ON THE ROAD TO EXHIBITIONS: PERFORMANCE
    ASSESSMENTS 27
    Checkpoints, Mileposts, and Backwards Planning 29
       Examples from the Field 31
          "Traditional" Curriculum Performed! 31
             A Science Lab and a Science Fair 32
             Social Studies Curriculum and
                Performance Assessment 47

Revisiting Performances, Reinforcing Skills
and Habits 54
Repeating a Format, Increasing the Challenge .. 60
Performance Assessments: What Do We Know? 62

3   EXHIBITIONS: SHOW WHAT YOU KNOW — FOR
HIGH STAKES 65
Traditional Curriculum, Performance Assessments 69
Turning Traditional Curriculum into Exhibitions ... 70
A Middle School Humanities Exhibition 77
Performances to Exhibitions: Three Systems 85
Common Threads — Learning from Examples 115

4   STANDARDS, CRITERIA, AND RUBRICS: INCLUDING
TEACHERS AND STUDENTS IN THE SEARCH FOR
QUALITY 117
Developing Local Standards for Quality
Student Work 119
Developing Rubrics and Scoring Criteria
to Define Standards 125
Teasing Out Quality through Rubric Design 126
The Pierre Van Cortlandt Middle School
Newspaper Project 127
The Fulton Valley Prep/Piner High School
Science Fair Rubric 129
Fulton Valley Prep/Piner High School
HEROES Exhibition Rubric 131
The Joel Barlow Writing Rubrics: Progress
Through Process 134
Standards, Criteria, and Rubrics 150

5   PSYCHOMETRICIANS AT THE GATES! ESTABLISHING
VALIDITY THROUGH DOCUMENTATION: A WORKSHOP
FOR CLASSROOM TEACHERS 153
Where Do We Begin? 156
Documentation: Triangulation and Beyond 166

BIBLIOGRAPHY 173

ACKNOWLEDGMENTS

More than most, this book really *does* owe a huge amount to other people. Because it is composed of examples *from the field*, I am indebted to all the teachers who contributed the work which made this possible. Their efforts in authentic assessment are leading the way into new frontiers in teaching and learning. I only hope these volumes to justice to their efforts.

Numerous others supported my work throughout the writing of this book and in the years leading up to it when I was exploring the use of new assessments. I have to particularly thank Grant Wiggins for his encouragement, honesty, and inspiration over the years. Likewise, the support and positive feedback from Heidi Hayes Jacobs helped shape many of the ideas which appear here.

There are too many people at the Coalition of Essential Schools to thank them all, but those who have had the patience and energy to always find time to listen and critique my work deserve mention. Paula Evans, Gene Thompson-Grove, Joe McDonald, Kitty Pucci, Kathy DiNitto, Pat Wasley, and Ted Sizer have been among that number. Colleagues with the National Re:Learning Faculty at the Coalition who have contributed ideas and support include Michael Patron, Carol Lacerenza-Bjork, Cheri Dedmon, Jude Pelchat, Dot Turner, and Steve Cantrell.

The Four Seasons Project at Teachers College, Columbia University, under the umbrella of the National Center for Restructuring Education, Schools, and Teaching, has provided me with another set of colleagues whose examples proliferate this book, as do many of their valuable ideas. Joel Kammer, Linda Quinn, Carol Coe, Linda Caldwell Dancy, Betty Kreitzer, Gary Obermeyer, Judy Onufer, Lynn Beebe, Millie Sanders, Jerry Howland, Rick Casey, Jan Hoff, and many other Four Seasons Faculty are among the finest teachers I have had the pleasure to work with over the years. Among the staff at NCREST, Linda Darling-Hammond, Ann Lieberman, Maritza McDonald, David Zuckerman, Kathe Jervis, Susan London, Rob

Southworth, and Terry Baker have all had a hand in shaping the work presented here.

I need to thank those friends in New York and Boston who have put up with eccentricities, idiosyncrasies, and general careening. In New York, Ilene Kristen, Ahvi Spindell, Jane Gabbert, Mandy Gersten, Anthony Angotta, John Chambers, Maureen Grolnick, Sherry King, Laura Lipton, Phil Kuczma, and Jay Fasold all had to listen to these ideas for years and years. In Boston, I received great support from Kathleen Cushman, Jamie Jacobs, Patti Jacobs, Charlie Berg, and Craig Lambert. I sincerely thank each of them.

Finally, I'd like to thank Bob Sickles, the publisher of this book, for his support and encouragement, his patience and guidance, and for believing in books like this. He is building a valuable library for educators of all levels.

Bil Johnson
Cambridge, MA
October 7, 1995

Author's Note

The Author would like to thank the following educators who have made contributions to this volume and have generously granted permission to include their materials:

Brown University Education Department
Providence, Rhode Island
    Larry Wakeford

Fulton Valley Prep, Piner High School
Santa Rosa, California
    Kathy Juarez, Humanities Team, and Science Staff

Heathwood Hall Episcopal School
Columbia, South Carolina
    Ted Graf, Marshall James, Dan Palma, and Staff

Bronxville High School
Bronxville, New York
    Linda Passman and Mary Schenck

Hibberd Middle School
Richmond, Indiana
    Randy Wisehart and Tammy Rhoades

Pierre Van Cortlandt Middle School
Croton-on-Hudson, New York
    Rick Casey

Joel Barlow High School
West Redding, Connecticut
    Jack Powers and Staff

FOREWORD

While America's educational leaders have long been devotees of testing, the current decade has unleashed a veritable flood of interest in and application of "assessment." The current prime question "Does it work?" arises both from a feeling of dismay about the quality of American schools and a stance of high distrust of the teachers and administrators who make up the system of these schools. Some of this testing craze is an affront, both to professionals and to scholars, who know full well the limitations of existing assessment "instruments" (the word itself says worlds).

What Bil Johnson has done in these two volumes is not so much to curse the darkness as to light some candles — turning assessment on its head by seeing it as a way to enliven and redirect teaching. Asking good "test" questions is simply asking good questions, the stock and trade of fine teachers and classrooms. The Socratic seminar not only goes back many centuries but both energizes the understanding of students and provides teachers with some sense of how those students' minds work. Johnson, a veteran teacher and scholar, has given us here a rich array of examples of the interwoven worlds of good teaching and reasonable assessment.

Throughout these books, Johnson's absolute trust in classroom teachers is powerfully implicit. Teachers will make a difference, not tests or the carrots and sticks which political leaders might attach to the results of those tests. Only teachers can both serve students in helping them to use their minds well and at the same time plumb those same students' work in a way that informs both students and structures, all the while presenting evidence of the larger world of where each students is and of whether his or her school "works."

These are books of helpful provocations. Those of us who teach will be stimulated by them, stimulated as Johnson would have us stimulate our students.

Theodore R. Sizer

INTRODUCTION

PERFORMANCE ASSESSMENTS: THE TERRITORY AHEAD

This is a book for teachers — particularly secondary school teachers. It is about an area within their immediate domain and requires their thoughtful, reflective, and energetic commitment. If teachers and students are not the central players in the performance assessment reforms which occur in our schools, there is probably no chance for that movement's success.

Performance assessment is *not* something which can be "learned" at a one-shot, "In-Service Day" inoculation — after which too many administrators and department heads charge their staff with implementation by Monday! Performance assessment *programs* must become part of a larger, ongoing professional development initiative which is designed to reshape the school as a learning community. This is a radical departure from what presently exists. This means reassessing the assumptions and goals of every member of the present community — from school boards, to parents, to teachers, to unions, to administrators, to students.

There are numerous books about those school redesign and restructuring possibilities (*see* Sizer, Schlecty, et al.). This book is about the practical steps teachers can begin, *with their students*, to reculture their classrooms and their schools — not an easy row to hoe. It requires hard work, making mistakes, taking risks, arguing with friends, second-guessing yourself, and a host of other problems. But it is aimed at keeping high quality student work *central* — a goal few schools remain true to at present — and it is designed to genuinely *empower* teachers to lead the way.

What should those students know and be able to do? How will teachers, parents, community *really know* what students have learned? In what ways will we assess their programs? Will we establish graduation systems which require performance and exhibition of student knowledge and ability and not just be a certification of school attendance? These are the questions *The Performance Assessment Handbook* addresses.

This book provides examples of work teachers are doing with their students *right now*. These are the pioneers in the *territory ahead*. The trails they are blazing are seldom straight and clean; some are deadends, while others terminate at a chasm or precipice. Yet they persist. And their students respond, joining them in this a new adventure. There is a vitality which Performance Assessments bring with them that is hard to describe because it doesn't fit the current paradigms of school. Classrooms are "busy" and noisy, students have a voice and have choices; teachers model risk-taking and lifelong learning behaviors, sharing their curiosity, questions, and confusion with their students. Parents are invited to join the process, to understand the goals of the journey, to support the teachers and students in their desire to find better ways to assess *genuine student progress* and more clearly define quality work.

The Performance Assessment Handbook is a guidebook, a travelogue, a suggestion, a provocation, an invitation, a journal, and a question mark. It is designed to encourage, incite, prod, present, probe, upset, cheer, and share. The audience can be teachers, students, parents, school officials, or any other citizens who care about our students. The hope is that conversations will follow, attempts will be made, questions will be raised, and students will be better served.

In the mid-1990s America is an emerging nation again. The world is realigned, the population's demographics are radically shifting, technology is accelerating at ever faster rates. The America of the '50s and '60s is barely recognizable — but that can even be said for much of the '70s and '80s, too. Think about the technology in your life which didn't even exist 10–15 years ago. Consider, too, what the political and economic world was like then. And then consider that the students in our schools today were, at best, *just being born*.

Cable TV (MTV!), personal computers, the end of the Cold War, the first signs of international globalism (European Economic Community, NAFTA, etc.), the new waves of immigration to the United States — these are a quick list of the world *today's* student has been born into or is growing up in.

The education system was designed in 1893, for an emerging industrial society with an increasing southern and eastern European immigrant population — an age in which the factory was the dominant symbol. Can we still say that about 1995 or beyond?

Performance assessment systems are the new path described in *The Performance Assessment Handbook*. This book is designed to help explore the world of the 21st century, to prepare America's students to be ready for change, to adapt to new circumstances, to understand the shifting landscapes of a world which *can't* be anticipated. This book is simply designed to help people find where that path starts. Once there, the road is theirs to create. Like anything new, it's a little scary and a little exciting. Decide for yourself. Try it — even if it's just a few steps down the path. Maybe create your own trail. You'll meet some folks along the way — they're all through the following pages — and they'll try to help you keep moving forward. One warning, though: Everyone we know who has traveled into the *territory ahead,* the territory *The Performance Assessment Handbook* describes, has never come back. The good news is that they are doing quite well, thank you, and they haven't come back *by choice.* This volume gives you a chance to meet them and find out why they've continued to pioneer new paths — and invites you to join them.

1

"Is This Going to be on the Test?"
Traditional Tests and Performance Assessments: The Territory Ahead

"Is this going to be on the test?"

People speak in code in schools. The simple question about "the test" has great meaning, and anyone who has spent time in America's schools knows what that question really means:

- Is what you're talking about *really* important?
- Should I bother to take notes on this?
- Is knowing this going to affect my future?

1

In much the same way, the teacher who says to the class, "Write this down; this is important," is basically answering the earlier question: this *is* going to be on the test.

The common point here is, of course, "the test." American students are the most "tested" in the world — in terms of standardized, norm-referenced tests. From the earliest grades, students are asked to match — pick "a," "b," "c," or "d;" select *True* or *False*, or fill-in-the-blank (often from a designated list of predetermined filler-ins) — on a wide variety of examinations. This is a 20th century phenomena, and has particularly gained momentum in the last 30 or 40 years. District, state, and national tests have become the yardstick by which students are ultimately evaluated. Indeed, a student's future is often determined by a single test score — the "fast" or "slow" reading group, the "accelerated" or "regular" math class, the prestigious private college or the state university.

This book is about performance assessments. It is not an argument for abolishing tests. It is a case for creating better "tests" and for using tests more wisely. It attempts to present its argument through the actual work of teachers and students who are already engaged in performance assessment methods — teachers and students who have struck out in a new direction, to understand better what students *really* know and are able to do as they move through their education. Before examining those assessments in detail, the context from which they arose should be better understood.

THE CONTEXT OF TODAY'S TESTING: WHERE DID IT COME FROM?

A key argument that arises throughout this book, and in any discussion about testing today, deals with the purpose of testing and, ultimately, the purpose of school. It is an argument as old as the American public school system. In the early 20th century, as the American public school system began to take shape, clear philosophical lines were drawn. On one side stood those who believed "science" would be the savior of humankind and that if humans could simply devise the correct (read "scientific") approach to their problems, those problems could be solved. The other side did not discount the value of science, but believed that some issues, particularly those associated with human development and discourse, could not be quantified or systematized so easily. While the debate raged, America was expanding rapidly, particularly in its urban centers, and the school system became the arena in which greater societal arguments were played out.

It was during the early decades of the 20th century that America emerged as a major world industrial power, largely due to development of "factory system" assembly line efficiency. The growth of the American economy had a tremendous impact upon the development of school systems — particularly in large urban areas. Some of the problems faced by the society (and, therefore, the schools) were: How do we socialize and inculcate a large immigrant population? How can we keep young people out of the workforce for a longer period of time, enabling older workers to find gainful employment? How can we "sort out" those people who are likely to be the best "managers" from those who are likely to be the industrial workforce? What is the most efficient way to answer questions such as these?

By the 1920s answers began emerging. As school systems began to imitate the hierarchical organizational structure of business (Superintendent's as CEO's, Principals as "middle management," teachers as "foremen" and "site managers"), the structure of schools themselves began to reflect the "factory system." Taking a cue from Taylor's studies on efficiency, schools became slavish imitators of "scientific management." The result was the system most of us know intimately — a system which still dominates America's schools: a fragmented curriculum delivered in cellular classrooms in which students are processed according to "grade level" until they either dropout or receive a diploma. Much of the "processing" is attained through testing. In essence, students are products traveling down a curricular conveyor belt — the English nut is put on, the Science bolt is tightened, a fender is added in Physical Education, and so on.

There are several premises upon which this system is based; premises based on assumptions which must be examined to fully understand how testing has come to have the importance and power it does in today's schools. But more significantly, we have to critically examine the foundations of the current system to understand why its premises may no longer apply to a nation headed into a new century.

- Premise #1: There is a known body of knowledge — the school's curriculum — which can be taught and mastered.

- Premise #2: Some students can learn that curriculum well, others not as well, and, still others, not at all.

- Premise #3: Dividing the curriculum (into subject disciplines) is an efficient and practical way to teach students.

- Premise #4: All people the same age learn at the same rate.

- Premise #5: Student understanding of school curriculum can be evaluated through standardized, norm-referenced tests.

There are more premises than these, of course, but this initial group provides a working context for examining why today's testing — and today's schools — need careful reexamintion and reform.

PREMISE #1: THERE IS A KNOWN BODY OF KNOWLEDGE — THE SCHOOL'S CURRICULUM — WHICH CAN BE TAUGHT AND MASTERED

While never entirely true (people's knowledge of the world has always been expanding), the idea that there is a quantifiable body of knowledge which students can master seems a ludicrous premise in a world of digital telecommunications. When one CD-ROM disk can hold 200,000 pages of double-spaced, typed information, one has to immediately question which knowledge on that disk is *essential* for students to know? And **who decides?** The need to develop "learning-to-learn" skills, based on a fluid and ever-expanding content base seems a more practical approach to curriculum. Yet, where, in the current testing system, can we discover if students have learned vital "learning-to-learn" skills? (*See* Wiggins, *The Futility of Trying to Teach Everything of Importance.*)

PREMISE #2: SOME STUDENTS CAN LEARN THAT CURRICULUM WELL, OTHERS NOT AS WELL, AND, STILL OTHERS, NOT AT ALL

If there is a genuine commitment to democratic schools and equal opportunity in this country, it is no longer acceptable to believe that only *some* can learn. Howard Gardner's work on multiple intelligences and recent developments and research in learning styles have clearly shown that *all* students can learn. The rub may be that they cannot all learn the same things, and they almost surely will not learn them all in the same way and at the same rate. This poses problems and challenges for educators, but also has serious implications regarding testing and assessment. The question is not, then, "How smart are you?," but "How are you smart?" — a very different perspective on student learning, certainly.

PREMISE #3: DIVIDING THE CURRICULUM (INTO SUBJECT DISCIPLINES) IS AN EFFICIENT AND PRACTICAL WAY TO TEACH STUDENTS

School is the only place where the world is fragmented into subject disciplines; the rest of life is an integrated experience. The negative effects of this structure are too many to mention, but a few glaring problems demand a word.

+ Teachers and students begin to see knowledge as isolated and discrete pieces of information, with little connection (and, often, little use) to anything beyond the immediate classroom experience.

+ Fragmentation requires short blocks of time for each subject — generally 40–50 minutes — preventing in-depth or sustained work. This also dictates how testing will be designed.

+ Communication between teachers — those in different disciplines and those at different grade levels — is almost nonexistent in most schools, resulting in a disconnected collage of subjects, topics, and work for students.

Beyond a rather grandiose "mission" or "vision" statement, school districts have no clear objectives for their graduates and, worse, no way of evaluating whether graduates have attained those objectives. Most diplomas, it seems, are simply certificates of attendance, reflecting little, if anything, as to what a student knows or can do.

PREMISE #4: ALL PEOPLE THE SAME AGE LEARN AT THE SAME RATE

There is no group of adults in any working situation who would blindly accept that workgroups or teams should be organized **solely** based on peoples' birth year. Yet, we do it all the time in school. In fact, despite all we know about cognitive development (Piaget's work has been accepted for well over half a century), we still do not hesitate to classify people according to their "grade level." The notable exceptions to this rule, of course, occur in the performance arenas in school — we would *never* keep the great sophomore running back off the varsity football team, or the excellent freshman oboist out of the school orchestra. Yet, those same students are rigidly segregated in their academics, even though we seldom know what kind of *performance* they are truly capable of because all we've done is "test" them periodically. Imagine schools actually establishing *performance checkpoints* for advancement to higher levels, rather than annual "moving up" exercises that reflect little regarding authentic student progress.

PREMISE #5: STUDENT UNDERSTANDING OF SCHOOL CURRICULUM CAN BE EVALUATED THROUGH STANDARDIZED, NORM-REFERENCED TESTS

Probably the greatest damage done by standardized testing is the pervasive negative effect it has on curriculum. Teachers teach "to the test." We know that. If there is a state-administered examination (like the Regents exams in New York State), or if there is a departmental examination given in a school (developed by whom and when?), we know that teachers will gear most, if not all, of their teaching toward that exam. So Advanced Placement American History courses spend hours and hours on details about the "facts" of U.S. history, so as to score well on the multiple-choice portion of the exam. And, even though they get a score back on the exam, they *never know* which questions they got right or wrong! But in a culture which cares only for the "definitive" score of a student ("Bobby's a 4;" "Karen got 1200 on the SATs") the concept of working for continued improvement — thereby **needing to know** what one missed and what one got right — is not important. And this is where standardized testing has probably had its most deleterious effect on American schools and its assessment practice. The point here is a simple one: We have created a system which is not designed to challenge students to *improve* performance over time. Simply going through the motions of leaping certain hurdles is enough — the quality of work, the degree of progress from their starting point to their present location is not what current assessments focus on. Genuine student progress and authentic achievement, then, are the victims of the current assessment system.

TESTING THE TESTS

One of the most important questions about tests has to do with their purpose: What are they designed measure or evaluate? With that in mind, a telling question teachers must ask themselves is this: If my students took my final exam *1 year later **without** my course "front loading" it*, how would they fare? Most teachers I know, when thinking about this question, have admitted that even their "best" students would probably score significantly lower, and that many would be dangerously close to failing. What does this tell us? Basically, that the students have spent much of the academic year working toward one goal, and once it has been reached, little is retained. In other words, they have actually *learned* very little. This also points out, again, how teachers will teach to a test, simply preparing students to do well in a one-shot performance, with little display of what they really might be able to do. If this is all we expect from students, this is what they will do. **You get what you test.** If, on the other hand, we ask students to solve complex problems requiring a number of skills which we can observe *in use*, our results will be far different.

The point is not that tests are inherently "bad;" the argument is not an either/or one. A straightforward, "traditional" test can serve some important purposes in school — particularly as feedback devices as to whether students have achieved the lower-order thinking skills of knowledge, comprehension, and application (refer to Bloom's *Taxonomy of Cognitive Objectives*). To determine whether students know geography, for example, a simple "fill in the map" or similar test or quiz provides a teacher with the feedback necessary to know if students have acquired knowledge, comprehended it, and can apply it. However, if we want students to move on to higher-order skills like evaluation, synthesis, and analysis, our assessment instruments will necessarily be more complex and demanding — for both the student and the teacher. Yet the present system is not designed to promote such assessment development. Let's consider an assessment system which is based on principles different than the those which currently dominate schools.

PLANNING BACKWARDS FROM OUTCOMES FOR CONTINUOUS PROGRESS

Richard Stiggins has pointed out that most educators receive little if any training in what he calls "assessment literacy." That is, beyond some simple statistics courses or psychometric principles for quantitative measurement, teachers are seldom taught to ask some simple questions: Why do we test? What is the purpose of the test? Who is the audience for the test's results? How will tests improve curriculum and instruction? Since the late 1980s the performance assessment movement has raised some important issues for consideration regarding testing and evaluation of students.

- ♦ What are the outcomes we desire for students? That is, what should they know and be able to do?

- ♦ Given those outcomes, what does *knowledge-in-use* look like? That is, if students are approaching or achieving those outcomes, what does their work look like?

- ♦ Assessment should be a tool for feedback, so that both teachers and students know where students stand in relation to the designated outcomes. That is, there should be a known continuum of progress upon which students and teachers can gauge progress, as well as evaluate the quality and effectiveness of curriculum and instruction.

- ♦ Therefore, assessment is an integral aspect of curriculum and instruction and **not** a separate event!

The challenge, then, is devising methods teachers can employ which will guarantee that assessments (the "tests" they teach to) will genuinely ask students to *use* knowledge in ways which reflect critical thinking, problemsolving, and other higher-order thinking skills, *and* which allow both students and teachers to measure student progress along with the effectiveness of curriculum and instruction in their school.

A crucial starting point in designing assessments is to begin with a clear picture of what it is we want students to *know and be able to do.* Unlike the 1970s movement for "behavioral objectives," though, this is not a simple series of "the student will . . ." statements. In the present context, what must be defined first regarding what students must know and be able to do (outcomes) is what those objectives look like in *performance* terms; that is, when students are engaged in their work, will they clearly show they "know" the scientific principle we believe is a significant outcome? The 1970s behavioral objectives, for the most part, simply asked teachers to teach, students to "keep up," and, at their best, to go back again and again to "master" an objective. The objectives were very often discrete snippets of information or a skill detached from any real-world application. Students were seldom taught for transfer; that is, asked to apply the skills or knowledge in a variety of contexts to actually show they genuinely *learned* the objective. Because most behavioral objectives were "tested" in one-shot, short-term multiple choice or fill-in examinations, there was little room for students to show whether they could actually apply ideas, concepts, knowledge, or skills beyond the immediate test situation.

Planning backwards from outcomes requires a more complex approach to assessment, curriculum, and instruction. In defining outcomes, the concept of *knowledge-in-use* must always be considered. This does not mean that everything taught must be "relevant" — it means that whatever the outcome is, it should be conceived of in terms of *what it looks like* when students are actively learning and applying the knowledge, skill, or concept. Two attendant factors arise here: First, when deciding upon outcomes (what students should know and be able to do) it is important to distinguish between skills, content, and attitude/disposition outcomes. Second, a school's (and often district's) curriculum needs to be critically reexamined. Because of the fragmented nature of curriculum and the generally poor communication which exists between teachers in schools (a factor the fragmented curriculum *promotes*), there is a great deal of redundancy for students, repetition of subject matter, and, in fact, *too much* reliance on pure content as the basis for curriculum.

In considering new assessments, the most significant **shift in basic thinking** which teachers, students, parents, administrators, and communities need to be willing to engage in is a reexamination of curriculum with the thought in mind that *things will have to go!* Because the culture of secondary schooling in this country has been one of **content coverage** for almost a century, this is a very difficult paradigm to shift. Yet it is essential if new assessments are to be developed. The trade-off is a simple one: depth for breadth. If we, in fact, do believe students must become effective critical thinkers, we must be willing to acknowledge that such thinking requires time and *cannot* be achieved if we insist on careening through a curriculum from September to June.

By focusing on outcomes, we can actually streamline curriculum in some ways. For example, most teachers would share an outcome like "effective problemsolving;" they will teach students to be effective problem-solvers in whatever course they teach. Yet, few teachers have any idea which of their colleagues also teach "effective problem-solving" or how their colleagues go about it! Were a faculty to focus on the significant outcomes for their students, share those outcomes with each other, *and then discuss* those outcomes collectively, we might find a much more efficient — as well as much better integrated — curriculum in many schools. Such communication, with its inevitable revelation of points of confluence between outcomes, could well provide teachers the vital time they need to teach for depth.

If we are to plan backwards from outcomes, then, we must also consider that curriculum will have to be driven by questions and not by content. The "humanistic" reform movement of the early 1970s, exemplified by the work of Edwin "Ted" Fenton, in particular, and supported by such curricula as Lawrence Kohlberg's Ethical Issues in Decisionmaking, initially raised the issue of "cutting" content curriculum, and replacing it with inquiry-driven, question-based curriculum. The 1980s has seen this mantle draped most significantly around the work of the Coalition of Essential Schools, an organization which has gained a significant following promoting the use of Essential Questions as the driving force for curriculum, with Exhibitions and Performances providing the crucial assessment instruments for evaluating student progress. Many of the examples which follow have been supplied by Coalition schools, since these are schools which have been willing to take the risk of moving away from the traditional assessment system, in the belief that more has to be known about what students know and are able to do than a simple objective test can ever reveal.

ESSENTIAL QUESTIONS AND PERFORMANCE ASSESSMENTS

Traditionally, teachers — untrained in assessment development — have been told they will teach a subject (11th grade American History, for example) and have, without much thought, proceeded to teach that subject based on the content in a textbook or a state- or district-issued curriculum guide. Creative and independent minded teachers, of course, always deviate from these guidelines but the basic approach, whether in humanities or the math/science areas, has been to start with the "beginning" (early history, basic number theory, the "cell," whatever) and then plod through the year hoping to "cover" everything. The word itself is revealing — to cover. It evokes an image which is secretive, not revealing. Such an approach demands that the teacher be the center of attention and activity. The student role is necessarily passive. Given what we know about constructivist theory, about the activity necessary for anyone to learn, the content-coverage approach leaves much to be desired.

Regarding assessment, it dictates a system which is also unrevealing as far as student progress is concerned. Students either "get it" or they don't. The class does not wait for people to progress at their own rate, to integrate, synthesize, or internalize content, skills, or attitudes in their own fashion. And it seldom asks the student to actively demonstrate what he or she knows. As a result, students are "processed." They begin with 11th grade U.S. history in September, they are fed the data, they indicate on objective tests and some essays whether they "know" the covered material or not, and they either "pass" on to 12th grade or not. Has their work improved? Have they truly understood significant concepts about interpreting the Constitution or American foreign policy? Does the teacher *really* know if they have? Does the student? And, ironically, the class has probably not reached the present day — where an opportunity to apply the lessons of history to the modern world might actually reflect what the student has learned. And that's American History. What of Global Studies or Western Civilization, with its millennia more to "cover?"

It is easy to criticize this curriculum, of course, when presented in such light. Yet the criticism raises a serious issue: What should students know and be able to do regarding American History? What is *essential*? And this is where planning backwards from outcomes departs radically from the current approach to schooling. If, in fact, we can clearly decide there is a manageable number of outcomes in the skills, content, and attitude areas which we want ALL our students to know and be able to do by June, we can begin to focus our curriculum much more intelligently and efficiently. We can also consider designing our curriculum around questions which promote *student* inquiry and activity, and engage the students as the actors, asking teachers to provide coaching, not facts. It also demands that assessment of student progress become integral to curriculum and instruction right from the start of any unit, course, and school year. Let's examine a hypothetical case study of a "backwards planned" curriculum driven by Essential Questions with assessments "built in."

A DIFFERENT APPROACH

What should students *really* know and be able to do after taking an American History course? What *is* essential to know and do? To pretend there is one simple and known answer to this question subscribes to the first premise and assumption discussed earlier — that there *is* a definite, known body of content which students should master. In 1995, I would contend we might consider the following design for an American History course, starting with identifying our outcomes, designing assessments which would reflect whether students have attained our outcomes, and creating essential questions which will drive our curriculum toward those assessments and outcomes.

AMERICAN HISTORY COURSE OUTCOMES, 1995

♦ *Skills Outcomes*

- Communication skills — reading, writing, speaking, & listening in a variety of styles and contexts.

- Data gathering , analysis, & interpretation skills — the skills of the social scientists and the historians. How do we put a story together and tell it? What is "the truth" about history?

These two skills areas alone represent a substantial curriculum foundation and a significant challenge for the classroom teacher/curriculum-designer and assessor. Focusing specifically on what kinds of readings and writings, what levels of development in speaking and listening skills, and *how to* assess student progress in those areas is quite substantial for a single year's curriculum. Add to that the skills necessary to work with primary and secondary sources, as well as applying the techniques of a variety of social science approaches to problem solving, and the core of an impressively challenging curriculum emerges.

- ♦ *Content Outcomes*
  - The Constitution: What does it say and what does it mean? How is all of American politics and American political history derived from how the Constitution is interpreted? The role of the Supreme Court and its decisions. What is democracy anyway?
  - A Nation of Natives and Immigrants: Who is an American? And by what right? How many American Dreams exist and who creates them? Listening to the unheard voices of American history — then and now. And where does democracy come into play for individuals and groups of citizens?
  - The American Continent: How has geography influenced people, politics, the economy? How does land create problems and solutions? How do natural resources shape values, create economies, influence politics? Can geography effect a concept like democracy — and if so, how?
  - The U.S. and World Affairs: from stepchild to parent-guardian. What role has the U.S. played in world conflicts — political, economic, ecological, cultural? Who determines who the U.S. is in the world's eyes? Must the world be democratic — and if so, why?

By looking at content curriculum in these broad areas teachers can pick and choose those historic events which will evoke the deepest and highest quality student work. By driving the content through questions — some of which are presented above — the opportunity to cross-reference history (and other social sciences) with the present is always possible, creating a greater possibility for student engagement and immediate relevance.

♦   *Attitude /Disposition Outcomes*

The basic outcomes I would consider focusing on as attitude or disposition outcomes are similar to those the Coalition of Essential Schools classify as "Habits of Mind." Along with habits of persistence, curiosity, independence, respect, and sympathy/empathy, these would be the inclination to

- Discern viewpoint or perspective.
- Search for or demand evidence.
- Make connections between what has gone before and what we are doing now.
- Identify if ideas, concepts, thoughts are new or old — have we worked with this before?
- Look for or demand relevance in their work.

Creating daily work and assessments which continually develop and reinforce habits like these in students, is part of what performance assessment design is about at its core. The integral nature of curriculum, instruction, and assessment are best illustrated when considering the attitudes/disposition outcomes because these are the daily commerce of the classroom. Are we designing student-centered work which will develop and reinforce these habits on a regular basis?

DESIGNING ASSESSMENTS WHICH EMBODY THE OUTCOMES

The next challenge is to develop assessments which will actually show what students know and can do in relation to the stated outcomes. And here again the break from traditional curriculum→ instruction→testing is most obvious. We are no longer simply starting with 1492 and proceeding chronologically to the present, periodically testing the material covered. By examining the outcomes we want our students to attain, our assessments begin to take shape and the appropriate content necessary for achieving our ends emerges. Given the four broad content outcomes, for example, we can consider spending an entire quarter of the year on each, applying the skills and attitude/disposition outcomes accordingly.

In examining the Constitution, for example, we would have to consider what it is we want students to know and be able to do to demonstrate their understanding of how that document has influenced American history, how it still effects contemporary politics, how it has been at the center of political development (and battles) for over 200 years. How could students exhibit such knowledge? Consider what students would have to know and be able to do to fulfill the following assignments. Also note how, in the process of meeting the objectives of each assignment, students would *have to* work toward mastery of skills and attitude/disposition outcomes.

◆ You are a delegate at the Constitutional Convention in 1787. You represent the state of (x) (different students would be assigned different states). Your state has certain economic and political interests which will be effected positively or adversely by the passage of the new Constitution. Prepare a position paper which presents your state's views on the new document, specifically comparing it to the Articles of Confederation and defending the Articles or the Constitution as an extension of the principles of the American Revolution. Refer to the Federalist papers in your paper as support, or as spurious, misleading arguments. Make sure you are clear about your position regarding the necessity for a Bill of Rights: Do you support or oppose the idea as essential to the ratification of the Constitution? Be prepared to present your state's case in formal debate, countering those who oppose your position and garnering the support of those who agree with your basic stance. If necessary, present other historical documents, maps, or visual aids which will make your case most convincing. Also: write a persuasive Letter to the Editor of the *Philadelphia Gazette* to win public support for your position. Finally, be prepared to vote for or against the ratification of the Constitution after hearing the open debate on the subject.

An assessment such as this, quite clearly, will require students to meet not only some of the content outcomes specified above, but also a number of the identified skills and attitude/disposition outcomes. The questions which might drive this "unit" on the Constitution could be one like: What is a fair and just government — and who decides? Another assessment, which would address that question while meeting another of the Constitution unit outcomes might look like this.

♦   You will be randomly assigned the role of a Supreme Court Justice. It may range from John Marshall to Stephen Breyer. As that Justice, you will have to write three opinions which indicate whether you are a strict or loose constructionist. The class will be divided into four large groups, each with a different set of three cases each. The strict and loose constructionists from each group (evenly divided) will argue their opinions on one of the three cases before the other three groups. The observing groups will have access to the Justices' opinions on the unargued cases before they cast their votes, supporting one side's arguments or the other's. The cases we will investigate will include the *Cherokee Indian* removal case, the *Dred Scott Case*, the *Standard Oil* case, *Plessy v. Ferguson*, the *Warren Bridge* case, *Fletcher v. Peck*, *Brown v. the Board of Education*, the *Miranda* decision, the *Bakke* decision, *Roe v. Wade*, the *Koramatsu* case, the *Pentagon Papers* case, and, of course, *Marbury v. Madison*. You may use other cases as references to support your opinions.

Obviously, students will have to meet all the communications skills outcomes, as well as many of the data gathering, analysis, and interpretation skills, along with most of the habits of mind attitude/behavior outcomes. All these are embedded in the content outcomes assessment and are driven by the essential question already mentioned: What is a fair and just government and who decides?

As this Constitution unit proceeds, students would have to construct timelines, determine historical context, make connections regarding cause and effect, select appropriate historical evidence beyond the immediate assignment, and make numerous interdisciplinary connections to their work. Consider the richness of such a curriculum compared to the usual chronological survey most of us have lived through. Will facts be missed or omitted? Quite possibly. Will students have a far greater *working* knowledge of the American system of government while developing reading, writing, speaking, and listening skills and habits of mind? Most definitely. What is most significant here, of course, is what the students will *show* about what they have learned. The focus is on *student performance and achievement,* student progress in demonstrable exhibitions — a quantum leap away from quantifying students with a simple score.

Let's consider the "Nation of Natives and Immigrants" segment of the curriculum next. Given the growing concern about and awareness for multicultural education, this is an important content area. How might students learn about multicultural contributions in American History and how could they show what they know? Here's one possibility.

◆ The textbook company which published our book realized they made several serious omissions. They are sponsoring a "Volume Two" contest and we are going to enter it. The class will be divided into teams, each of which will write a chapter to create "Volume Two." Each team will research one of the following groups: Native Americans, African-Americans, Latino-Americans, Asian-Americans, Disabled Americans, and Women. We don't want to create a superficial "survey" about any of these people, though, so our chapters will be aimed at answering important questions which will reveal what your group decides is most important to know about the people you are studying. Include primary source documents in your chapter (maybe as sidebars, maybe as text). Consider the following questions to drive your research:

• Do societies or communities need an "other" or an "outsider" in order to define themselves? How has your researched culture played the role of the "other" or the "outsider" in America, and how has that affected your researched culture? Consider — do any of these cultures discriminate against each other to create the "other" scenario? Is this a necessary component of community-building? Can it occur without creating conflict or harming others?

- Can immigrant, aboriginal, disabled, ethnic, or feminist cultures assimilate to "mainstream society" without losing parts or all of their own culture? Why or why not? And how so, or how not?
- Why is it important to understand your researched culture in the context of modern American society?
- Who should we know about from your researched culture, and why? What significant contributions has your researched culture made to American society that we should know about (and probably don't)? Create a timeline which notes important people and events, to create the historical context for the class to consider.
- What do you think your researched culture's "American Dream" might be? What is their view of democracy in America — and how does that compare with your own, as well as that of any of the other groups and/or the "mainstream" definition?

Each team should be prepared to present the class with its written chapter (complete with pictures, political cartoons, maps, graphs, charts, as appropriate) and to give a brief (one class period) summary presentation about not only the chapter content, but also **how** and **where** you researched your material. Individuals in each group will have to assume responsibility for focusing on one of the foregoing questions and researching it thoroughly. Organize your groups carefully, making sure everyone is clear as to what his or her assignment is, when due dates/deadlines must be met, and what the quality of work is which the group expects to achieve. (The class will develop criteria regarding quality work, but your group should come into that discussion with ideas in mind — what does excellent writing in this style look like? Can you find examples to share?)

By pursuing this research through initial, essential questions, students will have to raise more questions, developing their own role as inquiring researchers. Larger questions like, "Can America ever achieve genuine democracy?," will raise deeper issues for discussion, which will carry well beyond the classroom and also dovetail with the earlier work on the Constitution. Again, it is *the questions* and the assessments (designed to meet the stated outcomes) which are driving the curriculum. And, again, students *would have to be using* the skills described in the outcomes, as well as exhibiting many of the attitude/disposition outcomes, to complete this assessment successfully.

Over the past several years many citizens, as well as educators, have expressed concern that students seem to have little or no working knowledge of geography. One way to incorporate that content area into a study of American history is to involve assessments like those described next.

♦ Imagine it is the 25th century and you are a real estate agent for Century 25, an agency which sells property throughout the Solar System. Your "hottest property" is the third planet from the Sun. People from other galaxies are interested in large blocks of land (not quite continent size, but substantial amounts of property — hundreds of thousands of acres at a time). Your buyers are **only** interested in the natural resources an area has to offer (mountains, trees, rivers, potential farm land, etc.). By researching the geography and topography of the Earth, determine your two "top properties" and be ready to present a convincing "sales pitch" to your potential buyers. You may consult with classmates on this project, but each person will be responsible for presenting a 5-minute "sales pitch" with a one-page fact sheet on each of the properties she or he is selling.

While this assessment might raise some immediate concern from students — how do we know what the Earth will be like in the 25th century? What if the ozone layer is gone by 2400? — they can be instructed to indulge in "willing suspension of disbelief" and to consider the Earth as it is now — and maybe even in an improved condition if environmental consciousness continues to grow. Consider the *questions* students will have to generate to fulfill the assessment — and the research they will have to undertake to answer those questions! The teacher can then help the students focus on "macro"-geography, examining the U.S. position in North America, with all its resources and how those resources have been used, abused, or even ignored.

To examine the "micro"-geography of the U.S. itself, they could do the following:

♦ Each student will draw two states at random — they will be geographically contiguous — for this assignment. Your challenge is twofold:

   1. Create a brochure which will "sell" your states to as wide a variety of interest groups as possible: tourists, business people (in a broad number of fields), families, politicians, religious groups, ethnic groups, and so on. Focus on the strengths of your states — their location, their natural resources, their human resources, their economic strengths, their histories. Include any important statistics, charts, graphs, and so on. The brochure should be as attractive and informative as possible.

   2. Be prepared to "sell" your states to a panel of outside judges. We will be bringing in members of the community, parents, school board members, other teachers, town officials, etc., to hear your presentations and give you a rating. (We will devise the rating sheet in class. It will focus on the importance and accuracy of content, as well as the persuasiveness of your brochure and presentation.) You will also have to be prepared to field questions from the class. Remember, other states will be competing against yours, so people will have done enough research on your states to raise "Achilles heel" questions, trying to make you look bad and their states look good. Be prepared to defend your states **AND** to ask tough questions (not take cheap shots) of others.

   You will keep a nightly journal which lists your research sources and provides a daily reflection of what you are learning about the states you are researching. Your journal will also be where you record the questions you will ask of other presenters.

While this assignment will initially focus students on natural, human, and economic resources states have to offer, consider the deeper questions they will have to ask about government and politics — as well as greater questions about the "United" States and the

Federal government. Is it feasible to work with a multilevel system of government (federal, state, local) as we move into the 21st century? Should the U.S. divide into regional confederations to better serve economic needs and ends? What of those states which border Canada and Mexico — should they have "special" relationships with those countries above and beyond Federal agreements? So, while students will be studying geography at one level, the depth an assessment such as this demands requires students to actively probe for more information than that which initially meets the eye. And, again, students would *have to* be putting the skills and attitudes delineated in the outcomes *to use*.

Finally, our course asks students to consider the U.S. in world affairs, in both historical and contemporary contexts. The assessments we could use to prompt their activity might look like this.

♦ George Washington's *Farewell Address* (1797) and *The Monroe Doctrine* (1823) guided American foreign policy until World War II. Examine each of the following events and, in a well-organized research paper, explain how U.S. foreign policy conformed to or deviated from those policy statements. Conclude your paper by speculating how U. S. history might have been different if policy-makers had conformed to or deviated from the guide-lines set out by Washington and Monroe. Be prepared to discuss Washington's *Address* and Monroe's *Doctrine* in Socratic Seminars.

Events to Investigate — The War of 1812, the Latin American Independence Movement of the early 19th century (Simon Bolivar, et al.), the Civil War (relations with Great Britain), the Spanish-American War, World War I.

While this assignment seems to focus on wars, the student's research will have to concentrate on the concept of cause and effect and, more importantly, will have to apply the higher-order thinking skills of analysis, synthesis, and evaluation regarding U.S. actions in each instance. Previous units on the Constitution (role and powers of Congress and the Chief Executive), geography (who wanted what land and why), and U.S. attitudes and actions toward "nonmain-stream" ethnic populations would create a broad knowledge base from which students would conduct their research. In investigating modern U.S. foreign policy, students would be asked to do the following:

- ♦ Since World War II the United States has struggled with its foreign policy, often trying to be the "Good Neighbor" but coming across as "The Ugly American." In teams of four or five, you will develop a position paper for an address to the United Nations General Assembly entitled, "U.S. Foreign Policy, 1945–1995 — a Half-Century in Search of World Peace." You will focus on U.S. relations with regions of the world: Latin America, the Middle East, the Far East, and Eastern Europe and the former Soviet Union. Your group must decide how to present the U.S.'s case: Will you admit to errors and explain why they occurred or will you try to defend U.S. policies with an explanation of the "greater vision" of world peace America has tried to maintain? You may want to consider presenting both points of view, depending upon which region of the world you are focusing on. Each team will briefly present their position paper as an introductory exercise to a class analysis of U.S. foreign policy over this period, in which we will share our findings and try to conclude for ourselves what U.S. policy has been over the past half-century. After the class discussion you will, once again, select one area of policy (one region, perhaps) to write a "what if . . ." reflective essay, speculating on how things might be different if U.S. policy had been different.

The core of this assessment is somewhat "traditional" — do research, write a paper, have a class discussion, write another paper. Yet, there are some significant differences: the groupwork component addresses a number of skills and attitude/disposition outcomes; the research *requires* students to analyze and interpret events, not simply record them or list them; the conjecture paper will reveal how much students have synthesized, beyond simple comprehension and application of knowledge.

The Larger Context

This hypothetical case study of a revised American History course raises a number of questions which must be addressed — questions which are crucial to designing a performance assessment system and questions which respond to the concerns raised by moving away from a traditional content-coverage system. Because I have focused on American History, questions will also be raised about the possibility (or impossibility, some might say) of using this approach in other disciplines — particularly math or science. These are serious questions which must be addressed and not dismissed out of hand. But first, let's discuss this new assessment approach in a larger context — how does the school year proceed with this new curriculum, using assessments like those presented above?

Checkpoints and Mileposts

The assessments presented above would be equivalent to "unit tests," "midterms," or "final" exams which would be given in a traditional assessment system. As mentioned earlier, an important reason for devising a performance assessment system is to allow teachers to "teach to" more complex and meaningful "tests" for their students. Connected to this idea, performance assessments, because of their design, allow teachers to better plan curriculum and instruction based on those "tests." Students must be given time to learn how to work in groups, to present their work publicly, to do research with depth, to develop inquiry skills, and so on. For students to perform well on any of the assessments which are presented above, they need time to learn skills, to practice those skills, to rehearse presentations, to write and rewrite reports, and so on. Because teachers know (and there's no reason the students shouldn't also know) what the expectations for the students are (the assessments based on the outcomes are already designed), instructional activities and "minor" assessments (building blocks toward the large-scale assessments) can be designed systematically.

If we consider each of the assessments described earlier as *mileposts* students will reach as the school year progresses, teachers can then design appropriate *checkpoints* — those activities and exercises which prepare students for the Milepost Assessment and which serve as lesser assessments themselves. Checkpoints are those activities which allow both the teacher and student to gauge a student's progress toward successfully completing the Milepost Assessment. In this way, curriculum, instruction, and assessment are all of the same cloth; students and teachers work together, searching for answers to essential questions, solutions to problems, developing skills to apply — all the while using content as the vehicle which drives the work. The larger design of our hypothetical American History course, then, would look like this:

Milepost Assessments

- ◆ Early October — Constitutional Delegate Assessment.
- ◆ Mid-November — Supreme Court Justice Assessment.
- ◆ Late January — "Volume Two" Assessment on Immigrants, etc.
- ◆ Early March — Century 25 Real Estate Assessment.
- ◆ Late March — States Brochure and Sales Pitch Assessment.
- ◆ Late April/Early May — *Farewell Address/Monroe Doctrine* Assessment.
- ◆ Mid-June — U.N. Position Paper Assessment.

These dates would be flexible, of course, but they provide the teacher with an overview of assessments which facilitates planning the rest of the year.

For example, if the Constitutional Delegate Assessment is going to occur in early October, what must students learn, as far as skills, content, and attitudes, during September, so as to be prepared for that assessment? What are the ways the teacher will find out if their research is being done? Simply put, a **Checkpoint Assessment** on the *Federalist Papers* will be assigned by September 17th. Students might be asked to read *Federalist Papers* numbers 2, 6, 17, 25, and 30, and write a brief summary of each, with their own reactions or comments as their state's delegate. In class, the student then might present that writing (in his or her own words, **not** reading verbatim from the homework) to a small group of peers, for questions and answers, critiquing, and so on (**Checkpoint Assessment #2**). In this fashion, an entire series of activities can be designed, all of which help a student accomplish the **Milepost Assessment** with success, and at the same time move the student toward achieving the skills, content, and attitude/disposition outcomes which the course is designed around. In the larger context of the school year, then, focusing on outcomes, designing assessments, and creating driving (essential) questions to spur student inquiry, a teacher lays the foundation for developing the day-to-day exercises, assignments, and activities (revolving around small-scale **Checkpoint Assessments**). Most significantly, curriculum, instruction, and assessment are ongoing and integrated, creating a more coherent and fluid experience for students.

You Can't Do That in My (Math, Science, Health, etc.) Course . . . .

Many early performance assessments were developed in the Humanities areas. Because of that, and the assumption that Mathematics and Science *have to be* taught in a certain sequence, there has been slower development of performance assessments in these areas (even though some schools have been using performance assessments in *all* disciplines for almost a decade). With the advent of the National Council of Teachers of Mathematics Standards in 1991–92, and with similar standards now available for Science teachers (Science Benchmarks), the expectations in Mathematics and Science are clearly shifting. Expectations and concerns about advances in technology, as well as the U.S.'s stature in the world economy as the 21st century approaches, has contributed to a reassessment of *how* Math and Science should be taught, as well as *what* Math and Science students need to know and be able to do. In the course of this reassessment, a growing body of performance assessments, methods, and approaches have emerged. Examples of some of those assessments appear throughout later chapters of this book, and the Bibliography includes numerous texts which explore many of these new directions in Math and Science. The point here is that performance assessments are not exclusive to any one discipline — they are part of a greater movement which folds assessment into the development of curriculum and instruction.

PERFORMANCE ASSESSMENTS AND THE TERRITORY AHEAD

Adopting new methods is always difficult, and, in the case of performance assessments, the repercussions of change are far-reaching. It is an area which requires planning, thoughtfulness, and reflection every step of the way. Without those elements, and a commitment to improve what *teachers know* about what their students know and are able to do, the performance assessment movement will go the way of many other reforms of the past 30 years — half-tried, partially implemented, never fully understood. Our students deserve more than that. They need to know what the outcomes and expectations for them are and how they will be assessed. We need a system which addresses the numerous learning styles, abilities, and intelligences of *all* our students. Performance assessments are a first step in that direction; a first step on a journey in new territory. Michael Fullan says that change is a process, not an event, and the Coalition of Essential Schools likes to portray the change process as a "marathon, not a sprint." Changing the assessment system which has developed over a century will not happen quickly — but it has already begun to happen. Every teacher, administrator, parent, board of education member, and concerned citizen must, *at the very least,* begin to ask himself or herself what it is we expect our schools to do for our students and *how* we expect them — and us — to see the results of their education. Performance assessments are the beginning of that reflective process and that change process. A look at examples of what teachers and students are already doing in their classrooms reflects how far this movement has already come.

2

On the Road to Exhibitions:
Performance Assessments

The term "performance assessment" can be applied generically to any of the varieties of performance assessments employed — portfolios, exhibitions, Socratic Seminars, and even things like essays, laboratory experiments, classroom debates, or role-plays. In an effort to systematize our understanding of performance assessments, however, the use of the term *performance assessment* will have one distinguishing characteristic — it is an assessment used to gauge student progress *on the way to* an Exhibition presentation. As referred to earlier, *performances* are those **checkpoints** which enable students and teachers to assess student work as it builds toward a **milepost,** the Exhibition. In a traditional system, the *performances* would be those tests and quizzes, essays and assignments, which lead to the end-of-the-quarter, midterm, or final examinations. The crucial difference these *performances* introduce, beyond the "show-what-you-know" aspect of performance assessment, is the impact they have on curriculum development and implementation.

We know that tests and testing drive curriculum. In New York State, for example, the Regents examinations become the *total* focus for courses in all the "major" disciplines, as well as foreign languages and other courses. Teachers feel compelled to "teach for the test." In many cases, a teacher's success is judged by how well the students do on this one exam. Districts carefully eye each other's scores to see how they "measure up." Even though most teachers, parents, and administrators would admit that student scores on the exact same exam *taken 1 year later* (without the September-to-June "prep" course) would fall considerably, there is still formidable resistance to implementing other methods of assessment (as proposed by the recently-resigned Commissioner of Education in New York, Thomas Sobol). This highlights the difficulties which one will invariably face when starting a performance assessment system. Nonetheless, the goal is not necessarily to shift the idea of "teaching for the test." The goal is to teach to a new kind of "test" — one which is more thoughtful and requires more active and deeper work by students.

Imagine, if you will, students in New York State being asked to prepare for the Regents *Exhibitions* in June! How might that change the September-to-June teaching and learning in classrooms across that State? Most obvious would be the use of *performance assessments* as the primary means for checking student progress toward that final Exhibition performance. Because Exhibitions require a variety of tasks to be performed in answer to a complex problem, *performance assessments* throughout the year would provide students with the opportunity to prepare, to rehearse, to learn the skills and processes necessary to be successful. What that means, then, is that **curriculum** must change. It must be geared toward not only the final Exhibition, but also to creating *performance tasks* which students will have to engage in throughout the year. Once again, we return to the concept of planning backwards from outcomes to inform our curriculum development, implementation, and assessment designs.

CHECKPOINTS, MILEPOSTS, AND BACKWARDS PLANNING

The basic building block for curriculum in any performance assessment system is the *performance assessment*. The overarching goals — clearly defined outcomes in skills, content, and attitudes which are presented in culminating Exhibitions — define the destination of the curriculum. *Performance assessments* are the pathways to that destination, operationalizing curriculum and providing students and teachers with those **checkpoints** which gauge progress toward the Exhibition **milepost**. So, once again, it is the *process of planning backwards from outcomes* which creates the framework for redesigning curriculum, instruction, and assessment. And, unlike a traditional system of preparing for one test which is primarily content-oriented, the checkpoint/milepost framework is one which respects the integral *connections* between teaching, learning, and assessment. It reconfigures the teacher/student/content model by introducing the element of student *performance*, which must reveal what students actually know and are able to do. This shift is crucial, of course, because it doesn't simply introduce a new element — it introduces an element which has a domino effect on the existing trinity. When the concept of *student performance* becomes part of the classroom equation, everything goes back to Square One.

Once the commitment has been made to advance students according to the exhibition of knowledge and skills, the conception of curriculum and instruction *has to change*. By way of example, let's consider the Graduation Portfolios from the Crefeld School in Philadelphia and Central Park East in New York (*see* Volume 1) which were presented in the last chapter. What do students have to do to prepare for those exhibitions? What does the curriculum of the respective schools look like to prepare students for those final exhibitions? If we see those Graduation Portfolios, then, as the **mileposts** which students are striving to attain, consider what **checkpoints** will need to be along the way. They will have to be a variety of *performances* which allow students and teachers both to know when students are ready for their milepost "test."

Grant Wiggins has worked extensively in the field of performance assessments for a number of years now and has developed a list which helps define "performance" and makes clear how this system differs from a traditional approach. According to Wiggins, *"performance* implies:

1. a *repertoire,* not a simple 'response' to stimulus; it requires good judgment and adaptiveness, in light of a complex goal.

2. a 'whole' work that is more than the sum of its parts:
- fluid performance
- sum of drills.

3. opportunity to personalize: the work reveals 'voice,' style, or 'signature' (while solving the problems at hand).

4. rehearsals, refinement, feedback, and revision:
- known criteria and standards
- multiple opportunities to demonstrate control.

5. nonscriptable responses, not pat responses to exercises; mastery occurs via attention to criteria and standards, not to obeying recipes and step-by-step instructions only.

6. impact, not process, is the *key* criterion. Performance is typically judged:
- by the effect on a real audience — in a *specific* context
- whether it "worked" to achieve the performer's intent and/or the audience/consumer's expectation.

7. that an excellent performance may (likely) have minor errors
- the *response* to (and graceful/effective recovery from) error is often more important than the errors made.

8. eventual autonomy — the coach on the sideline — where the performer can self-adjust."

CLASS 1994 workshop publication, p. 20

These guidelines highlight the specific ways in which performance assessment is quite different from traditional testing or evaluating, with equally clear curricular implications. Wiggins's guidelines also provide an excellent framework to use in analyzing the *performances* which follow. And these examples from the field follow the process described throughout this book: focus on outcomes; devise an Exhibition (or Exhibitions–Milepost, "final" performances) which will enable students to show they have reached the outcomes; develop *performance-based assessments* (checkpoints) and curriculum which provide a clear path to the outcomes and the Exhibition.

EXAMPLES FROM THE FIELD

The performance assessments presented in the remainder of this chapter are designed to present the variety of ways teachers *in the field* have created checkpoints to insure student progress toward outcomes and exhibitions. In some cases, examples are presented from very "traditional" schools, where final exams that are highly content-oriented are still used as the milepost. Nonetheless, these practitioners have devised ways students can engage in *performance assessment* to deepen their knowledge of a subject area — not simply absorb and spew back content. And this raises an important point about the *transition* to a performance assessment system — very few schools will totally adopt a new assessment system overnight.

Most schools will adopt a "wait-and-see" attitude as several assessment pioneers venture out into this new territory. It is important, then, to recognize how we can adapt those elements of the existing system in ways that better serve the learning of the students. By "ratcheting up" the expectations for students — creating demanding performance assessments, for example — test scores will not suffer and students will leave with a deeper understanding of the subject at hand. As teachers increase the frequency of performance-based assessments, students begin to not only rise to those challenges but to expect — and sometimes *demand* — a more active and responsible role in the classroom. A number of the examples that follow will be clearly recognizable as content-connected to some very traditional coursework. What distinguishes these assessments is how their design requires students to become active learners, demanding they show what they know and can do in ways a "traditional" test could never measure.

"TRADITIONAL" CURRICULUM PERFORMED!

The first set of performance assessments from the field present a five examples of assignments connected to very traditional curriculum content. What sets them apart, as we analyze them with Wiggins's guidelines, is that they do require a repertoire of skills, yet allow for personalization. They "build-in" rehearsal, feedback, and revision, and are certainly not calling for "scripted" responses. They will have an impact on an audience, even if only in a classroom context. And they do all build toward student autonomy, particularly in developing critical thinking and problemsolving skills.

It should be noted again, however, that to implement the assessments presented here *within the bounds* of a "traditional" curriculum, some other content would, invariably, have to be deleted. Again, the focus is on the significant outcomes and *not* on content-coverage. The teachers in these situations made the decision for depth over breadth, recognizing the need for students to learn the importance of *probing* for solutions, *thinking through* problems, and finding original answers. That significant decision was followed by an important action — the design of an assessment which requires student performance to show both the teacher and student what has been learned.

A SCIENCE LAB AND A SCIENCE FAIR

Laboratory sciences are a field inclined toward performance assessment, yet, too often, students are presented with "recipe" labs in which they plug-in certain ingredients and write down, on predesigned forms, their "results" — with everyone expected to get the same answers. We know that authentic science is far from recipe-oriented and requires original work, problemsolving, hypothesis testing, and a basic trial-and-error approach.

Many secondary science teachers develop some of their own laboratory experiments for their students — genuine performance assessments. Yet, an equal number or more still feel the pressure to "cover the content" of the Biology or Chemistry or Physics textbook, and simply have their students go through the motions of laboratory experiments without ever really understanding the process scientists engage in. The following is a lab activity developed by Larry Wakeford (now a Clinical Professor in Brown University's Master of Arts in Teaching program) which takes the topic of natural selection and creates a laboratory simulation out of it (Fig. 2.1).

Setting up the lab tables with multicolored and multipatterned swatches of fabric (paisleys, checks, stripes, and so on, in a vast array of colors), students take on the roles of predators and prey to reach some conclusions about natural selection. Let's look at the assignment as it is presented to the students and then consider how this *performance* is a **checkpoint** assignment for students.

(Text continues on page 36.)

FIGURE 2.1: LABORATORY ACTIVITY —
NATURAL SELECTION: A SIMULATION

NAME _____   DATE _____   PERIOD _____

LABORATORY ACTIVITY: *NATURAL SELECTION--*
A SIMULATION

Biologists consider natural selection to be the chief mechanism of evolutionary change and the process responsible for the diversity of life on earth.   This investigation illustrates one way in which natural selection operates.

PROCEDURE
1. Spread out the fabric "habitat" on a counter top.

2. Examine the paper chips in your plastic bag and record the colors of the chips on the data chart.   There are 100 chips, 10 each of 10 different colors.

3. Appoint one team member as the keeper of the bag of chips.   All other members of the team are "predators", whose "prey" are the chips.   The keeper will keep track of the number of turns each predator takes and the number of prey remaining.

4. The "predators" should turn their backs to the counter and allow the keeper spread the chips uniformly over the fabric, making sure no chips stick together.

5. Imagine yourself as <u>predators,</u> the paper chips as your <u>prey,</u> and the fabric background as your <u>habitat.</u>   One at a time, turn around and select five chips using only your eyes to locate them.   Do not use your hands to locate the chips.   When you have selected the chips, place them in the cup, and then turn around.   Continue taking turns until only 25 chips remain on the fabric and the keeper signals you to stop.

6. Carefully shake the fabric to remove the survivors.

7. Group the survivors according to color by placing chips of the same color together.   Arrange them in a row.   Record the number of survivors of each color on the data sheet in the column labeled "1st round survivors".

8. Assume each survivor produces three offspring.   Using the reserve supply of chips that your teacher has, place three chips next to each

survivor.   Record the new numbers in the column labeled "2nd round start".

9. The keeper should mix the survivors and their offspring thoroughly and distribute them as was done in step 4.   Do not use the chips that were "eaten."

10. Repeat the entire process twice more if you have time.

11. When you are finished reestablish in the plastic bag the original 100 chips of 10 chips of each color for the next class.

12. Now you are ready to analyze your data.

ANALYSIS AND DISCUSSION

1. Was one color or colors represented more than others in the first generation of survivors?   Which color(s)?   Why do you think these chips "survived"?

2. What, if any, change occurred between the first and second generation?   between the first and fourth generation?

3. Compare the original and the last survivor population.   Which, if any, color from the original population is not represented in the survivor population?   Why?   To what event in real populations is this result comparable?

4. Examine the colors of chips in the fourth generation and the fabric habitat.   How do the colors of the survivors relate to the colors of the habitat?

5. How are your results related to the process of .natural selection?

6. If new individuals of different colors immigrate into your population, what will be the effect on the population, assuming that habitat and predators remain the same?

7. Compare your data to those of other groups.   Were the results the same?   How do you explain this?

(Adapted from Investigation 9.2 in <u>Biological Science-An Ecological Approach</u>, 7th edition by L. Wakeford, 10/94)

Natural Selection Lab Worksheet

COLOR	Original Population	1st round survivors	Population at start of 2nd round	2nd round survivors	Population at start of 3rd round	3rd round survivors	Population at start of 4th round	4th round survivors

LAB ACTIVITY AS PERFORMANCE

By examining what students *had to do* and then looking at what they were *expected to know* we can see how this activity is a performance checkpoint and not a "recipe" lab.

The expectation going into this activity is that students will have read background material about evolution and natural selection. Quite possibly, the teacher has made some kind of presentation or done some Socratic questioning with the students. But the purpose of this lab activity is for students to actually *understand* how natural selection occurs and draw their own conclusions. So, while a very "traditional" area of content is being "covered," students are also being asked to engage in a performance assessment which will deepen their understanding of a concept which is a content-outcome for the course.

Through the simple process of role-playing "predators" and "prey" operating in a "habitat," the students actively engage in understanding how natural selection works. The teacher is always available to answer questions or clarify procedures, but the students have to conduct the activity themselves and then, most importantly, *analyze* what has happened. Here we see how a skills-outcome is attained. Students will have to engage in the higher-order critical-thinking skills of analysis and evaluation because they are expected to present their results for comparison with others.

In role-playing this lab activity, students will also engage in several attitude-outcomes: working cooperatively with others (assigning roles, taking responsibility for that role, and so on), asking for help if necessary, and being confident in presenting results to others.

By framing this lab activity within those outcomes, we can see how a "traditional" content subject and a "traditional" classroom approach (a lab) can be transformed into a more student-active, constructivist activity. In this case, the students would be expected to not only conduct the activities of the lab, but also come to certain conclusions about natural selection (supported by data they collected) and compare those conclusions to their classmates. The opportunities for self-assessment (and speculation for self-correction) are apparent here and, most importantly, the focus on student *performance* in moving toward significant outcomes is clear. For those who would be concerned about the activity being conducted as a "group," the lab could easily be redesigned to work with the traditional "lab partners" paradigm. Whatever the student configuration, the point remains the same — students constructing knowledge through activity and performance are more likely to evoke higher-order thinking, while exposing the students to more authentic scientific work.

GOING TO THE FAIR

As with lab activities and experiments, the Science Fair is often present in schools, providing a perfect opportunity for students to engage in authentic work and to actually *perform* Science. But, again, too often, these Fairs become shows which invest far more in form than substance, seldom requiring students to actively defend or explain their work, and are done in a rather perfunctory fashion because of time and/or space considerations. It's a shame, really, because the Science Fair provides an excellent opportunity for students to engage in *performance* assessments in a highly visible arena, one in which they could actively learn a great deal.

Fulton Valley Prep is a division of Piner High School in Santa Rosa, California, and its science staff has created a Science Fair Exhibition, with several *performance* assessments which lead up to the Fair. Focusing on the physics of sports and recreation, some very traditional Newtonian physics content was placed in the hands of the students in several unusual contexts.

In this example, we will examine what *performance* assessment might look like from a student's point of view, while still considering the teacher's outcomes and curriculum development process.

GETTING HELP TO REINVENT THE WHEEL

Throughout the late 1980s, when schools were embarking on attempts at restructuring and reform, a common refrain heard in workshops and faculty meetings was, "Do we have to reinvent the wheel? Aren't there models out there?" The fact of the matter was that there were very few models "out there" and people did, in fact, have to blaze new trails in assessment, interdisciplinary work, restructuring, school-site management, and the whole array of areas restructuring entails. As we moved into the '90s, however, models did begin to appear and those interested in moving in new directions could learn from some of what had gone before. Fulton Valley Prep, a "school-within-a-school" concept which began in the early '90s with a commitment to follow the Common Principles of the Coalition of Essential Schools, is a good example of a school which looked at what was going on in the reform movement and adapted those ideas and concepts which they believed would help them implement their own brand of restructuring.

In developing their "Physics of Sports and Recreation" performance assessments (Fig. 2.2) for the Spring of 1994, the Fulton Valley Prep staff borrowed several ideas and built upon them to create a series of performances designed to culminate in a Science Fair Exhibition. Taking a cue from Central Park East's experience, the Fulton Valley Prep teachers framed their project around three basic questions: "Where are we going?" How will we get there?" and "How will we know when we've arrived?" In the same fashion, they adapted an assessment developed by Joan Boykoff Baron for the Connecticut Common Core of Learning — the Maplecopter activity — to introduce their students to basic Newtonian physics concepts. What we find in the Fulton Valley Prep Science Project, then, is an excellent mingling of traditional Physics curriculum (necessary content outcomes), with a focus on student *performance* through the adaptation of ideas which are "out there," combined with their own creativity.

By presenting students with the "Where are we going?," "How will we get there?," and "How will we know when we've arrived?" questions at the beginning of the project, the teachers established clear guidelines and expectations for students. Once again, students are expected to present their findings to the class, having actually engaged in "hands-on" experiments, using textbooks as references, and recording their work in journals. The responsibility for the project is clearly focused on student *performance*. The combination of short, in-class performance assessments with a longer-term exhibition project is a perfect example of how performances serve as **checkpoints** on the way to the **milepost** exhibitions. And, once again, what we find *included in the assignment* from the very beginning are clear guidelines as to what quality work would look like.

By giving students a "Rubric for Science Fair Projects," as well as guidelines for what should be in their journals, followed by a Reflective Writing assignment, the components for the assessment are clearly in place — students have a sense of what they should

(Text continues on page 46.)

FIGURE 2.2: FULTON VALLEY PREP —
PHYSICS OF SPORTS AND RECREATION

Fulton
Valley
Prep

Sciences Core
Spring, 1994

a 21st century
education

The Physics of Sports and Recreation

Where are we going?

Why and how do things move? Why do things fly, float, flutter, hover, fall? Why do balls bounce, curve, drop? What affects how far and fast objects move along inclined planes? Why do moving objects stop, and what forces affect whether the stop is abrupt or gradual, gentle or destructive? What are simple machines, and what forces affect the efficiency of those machines? What's the difference between a home run and a fly ball to the warning track? If struck by a baseball bat, which type of ball-- a baseball, a soccer ball, a golf ball, a tennis ball, a softball, a football-- would travel farthest, and why? Why do bobsleds look the way they do? What factors affect how high and how far ski jumpers travel? Why can Fosbury floppers high jump higher than Texas roll jumpers? Can Michael Jordan fly? Why are racing cars and airplanes designed the way they are? How can we design investigations and experiments to give us insight into these areas? These and other related questions will guide our work as we delve into Newtonian physics and observe, record, and analyze the rules which govern the physical world around us.

How will we get there?

We will begin by trying hands-on investigations into a number of areas such as ball games; flying things; egg drops; and cars. We will speculate about the reasons for observable physical phenomena and design ways to isolate specific factors and build models to test the importance and effect of those factors. We will study and look for applications of Newton's laws of motion, Bernoulli's Principle, and aspects relating to motion such as velocity, acceleration, air resistance, momentum, and centrifugal force. Through readings, videotapes, and Socratic Seminars, we will explore these and other aspects of mechanics and motion, and touch briefly on atomic and sub-atomic physics as well.

How will we know we've arrived?

The exhibition for this unit will be based an original investigation which illustrates the aspects of Newtonian physics as they relate to sports (or a sport) or recreation, and will consist of four parts (explained in more detail on a separate handout): 1) documentation of all your work and thinking on this unit via a notebook/collection of your planning, critical thinking, problem solving, and reflecting; 2) production of a "Science Fair" style display board presentation of your work; 3) design and assembly of a "product" for competition; 4) competition with other students who have designed products in the same category.

Fulton
Valley
Prep

Sciences Core

Maplecopters: A look at why things fly

"I am never content until I have constructed a mechanical model of the subject I am studying. If I succeed in making one, I understand; otherwise I do not."

--Scottish physicist Lord Kelvin (creator of the Kelvin scientific scale of temperature)

The Task:

Working with a partner: 1) carefully observe a natural phenomenon, the way in which a maple tree seed pod spins as it falls through the air; 2) hypothesize about the forces that affect the observed phenomenon; 3) decide which two of the possible factors or forces are the most significant; 4) construct models to test the hypotheses; 5) conduct the tests, again carefully observing and recording the results; 6) adjust your hypotheses based on the results of the tests; 7) present your findings to the class.

The Procedure:

•Choose a partner; in classes with an odd number of students (as opposed to classes with a number of odd students), there will be one group of three students.

•Select some seed pods. Choose a variety of shapes and sizes.

•Drop the seeds in a variety of different ways and from different heights. Observe the results. Write, describe, sketch as necessary to record your thoughts and ideas.

•Discuss with your partner the various forces at work, and which seem most important. Refer to the text (*Conceptual Physics*, especially chapter 4) as necessary for ideas and clarification.

•Using only paper and tape, construct a series of models to isolate facors that you would like to test for. Brainstorm ways to isolate these factors by varying the size, shape and weight of the models.

•Test the models by recreating the types of drops you did with the seeds. Change the models or build new ones as necessary to further isolate and clarify the factors you're looking at. Carefully observe, reflect, speculate.

•Discuss with your partner and come to agreement about the importance of the various factors you tested for.

•Present your findings to the class.

•Reflect in your notebooks on what the whole class did and learned about flight, stability, free fall, air resistance, etc.

Flying Things: Day Two

Before you do today's investigations, carefully read portions of chapter 20 in *Conceptual Physics*; specifically, study sections 20.6, 20.7, and 20.8.

Yesterday you observed the "flight" (or falling) of maple seed pods and attempted to build models of the seed pods and to determine what made them behave in the characteristic way they do when dropped. Today you will apply some of what you learned to the constructing of paper airplanes and the testing of your planes to see which factors make them fly father, stay airbourne longer, and otherwise affect flight.

The procedure:

(Important Note: Do not fly any of these planes until you are told to do so!!!)

- Build a paper airplane from a single sheet of 8 1/2" X 11" paper.
- Compare your plane with the others at your table. What features and characteristics do they have in common? What, if anything, is absolutely unique about your plane? Record observations (including sketches) in your notebook.
- Build another plane, this time a "standard model" as specified in the handout.
- Compare, record and reflect as above.
- Build a "canard" according to instructions on the handout. Do you know what the word "canard" means?
- Compare to previous two planes, record and reflect as above.
- Build a "Delta wing" and a "cylindrical wing" plane; as before, examine yours and your tablemates' work, compare the constructions and designs, and note and record similarities and differences.
- Make some predictions as specified on the top of the "Start flying" sheet. Besides predicting which plane will fly farthest, also predict which will fly straightest and which will stay in the air longest. Also write why you believe each of your predictions. Record all predictions.
- Fly 'em! Once all the planes have been built and all predictions made, put your designs to the test and record the results on the "Start flying" sheet.
- Analyze your results by comparing your predictions to your results. Reflect on what happened and what you learned from it.
- Fill in the "Ask some questions" side of the sheet. We will use your questions as the basis of the "debriefing" of the flying things portion of this unit.
- Add any closing ideas, reflections, speculations, or questions to your notebooks.

LONG TERM DESIGN EXHIBITION
"To Build a Better Mouse Mobile"

OBJECT: To build a vehicle which will travel as far as possible whose source of initial impulse is a single standard mousetrap.

RELEVANT SCIENCE:
Physics Chapter 3-8. *Energy, Motion, Newton's Laws: Inertia, acceleration, action/reaction, net force, momentum.*

DUE DATES:

Mouse Mobile

First Design Review (Detailed Drawing Only)	Tuesday, March 8
Second Design Review (Product)	Friday, March 11
Competition (Final Product and Final Drawing if Modified)	Wednesday, March 16

Science Show Information

First Information Review (Physics used in design of vehical)	Wednesday, March 9
Second Information Review (Science Show Board Review)	Monday, March 14
Final Science Show Exhibition Due	Wednesday, March 16

APPARATUS:

Design Limitations
- The only source of energy for each vehicle will be a mousetrap provided by your teacher, after you have submited and receive approval on your first design review.
- Each vehicle must carry all of its parts the entire length of the track, i.e. it may not use an object or part to help get it started then have those parts left behind.
- No electricity or electronic devices may be used in the solution. This eliminates electric fans, radio controlled devices etc.
- During the races you must remain behind the start line and may not interfere with your design.
- Your vehicle may not be longer than 5 ft., and wider than 2 ft.

THE COMPETITION
A course will be laid out in the GYM consisting of three tracks 2 feet in width. Tracks will be separated by a thin chalk line.   Three designs will race at a time. Each design will have a maximum of 2 minutes to set up the trap and release the spring. Designs must stay within the chalk lines during the entire duration of the race. Designs that cross over the chalk lines will be automatically lose the race.   The designs that travels the farthest distance will advance to a semi-final round and then on to a final competition round.

SCORING
For this exhibition you will be evaluated on three things: Your **notebook**, your **exhibition project**, and your **science fair information and display**.

For the "build a better mouse trap" portion of the exhibition you will be evaluated on:
1) Design reviews. (Detailed drawings, which must include the physics principals applied in your design.)
2) How well your machine works. (Distance traveled & path of travel.)
3) Quality of final product.
4) Bonus for creativity

Fulton Valley Prep

Sciences Core
The Physics of Sports and Recreation

Rubric for Science Fair Projects

Mastery:	Distinguished:
1. Display Board clearly reflects the product development process.	**Overall:** Display Board is striking, attractive, well-organized, thorough and shows careful attention to detail.
2. Display Board includes summaries of all experiments and the results, with appropriate illustrations, measurements, calculations,and graphs.	1. See *Mastery*.
3. Display Board includes a model or drawing of the final product.	2. See *Mastery*. Also, neatly written, thorough, in-depth summaries of experiments, including quantative data, measurements, calculations and graphs.
4. Display Board includes writeup with appropriate conclusions based on data.	3. See *Mastery*. Also, model or drawing is to scale, neat, clearly labelled, and detailed.
5. Display Board includes thorough explanation of the relevance of the principles of Newtonian physics to the performance of the product.	4. See *Mastery*. Also, conclusions show thoughtful and significant insight into the experimental results and data.
6. Notebook is a thorough record of the process of the development of the final product, including **lab writeups, answers to assigned questions, vocabulary exercises, and reflective writings** about the concepts, experiments and results.	5. See *Mastery*. Also shows clear connections between the performance of the product and the Newtonian principles involved.
7. Product exhibits care in thought, planning, and construction. Attention to detail is evident.	6. See *Mastery*. Notebook entries are thoughtful and in-depth and reflect clear insight into the connections between the experiments, readings, and concepts.
	7. See *Mastery*. Product also shows originality and creativity.

What Should be in Your Journal?

_____ Cover Page (B)

_____ Cover Page Typed (A)

_____ Table of Contents (B)

_____ Table of Contents Typed (A)

_____ Bibliography (B)

_____ Bibliography Typed (A)

Labs:
(Only five labs are required)

_____ Bounce, Bounce Bounce
_____ Bounce, Bounce, Bounce (Rolling Things)
_____ The Domino Effect
_____ Flying Things
_____ Balloons Rockets
_____ Egg Drop
_____ Maple Copters
_____ Other Lab

Homeworks:
(All homework is required for you to receive a grade)_

_____ Chapter 2
_____ Chapter 3
_____ Chapter 4
_____ Chapter 5
_____ Chapter 7
_____ Chapter 8 (Notes from this chapter)

Notes:

_____ Notes while developing your exhibition. This might include your first drawing of your exhibition, your notes as they relate to the physics involved in your exhibition, ect.

**Fulton
Valley
Prep**

a 21st century
education

Sciences Core
The Physics of Sports and Recreation:
Reflective Writing

Now that you've read, talked, questioned, watched, designed, built, tested, modified, competed, and displayed the results of your efforts, it's time to look back on the process and the learning that went on. In your clearest and best writing please tell me:

1) specifically what you did during the three weeks plus that we were engaged in this unit (not what was assigned, but what you_did). Include in how you spent your class time, how much and what type of homework you did, what you did as an individual and as part of a group, etc.; also include an evaluation: which activities, projects, investigations, writings, etc., did you find most meaningful and educational?

2) what you learned as a result of this unit. What do you know know about science in general and the physics of motion in particular that you didn't-know before we started? Please include knowledge about the process of research and product development, experimentation, testing theories, etc., as well as specifics of Newtonian physics.

3) Given your experience, what would you have done differently if you could start such a unit over again to make it a better and more meaningful educational experience? What should we have done differently in terms of curriculum, structure, content, scheduling, teaching, expectations, evaluation, etc.? Please explain your suggestions.

This piece of writing will be the last entry in your interactive notebook. Thanks for your work and your help in improving curriculum and raising standards in FVP.

know and be able to *before they begin* the performance tasks. Let's examine the assessment as it was presented to the students and then analyze how it improves upon traditional science lab and Science Fair conventions.

THE REINVENTED WHEELS

As with the earlier *performances* presented, what strikes one most in reviewing the Fulton Valley Prep assessments is not only the active role students must play in *understanding* the concepts being studied, but the *application* of textbook materials to actual use in the classroom. The assignment clearly instructs students to work their way through textbook chapters, but, most significantly, requires them to apply what they have read to actual experiments for deeper understanding. It also incorporates an element of competition and "play" (the Mouse Mobile races) which we might not always find in traditional classroom settings. The competition is based on the quality of the products the students create — a far cry from tests which pit students against each other in a test of memory or "plug-in" formulas and answers.

What is also notable in this series of performances, particularly in referring back to Wiggins's guidelines, is how much of these activities do not have "scriptable" answers, how students do have to apply a "repertoire" of skills, and how much "impact, not process, is the *key* criterion." It also allows for "rehearsals, refinement, feedback, & revision" and recognizes that minor errors may be part of "Distinguished" performance.

Another significant departure from traditional modes of teaching, learning, and assessment presented in this example is the Reflective Writing piece at the end. First and foremost, let's consider how often students are asked to write in Science classes, in general, beyond filling in "lab reports." Including this component makes a clear statement about the work of scientists and the pursuit of science as a thoughtful and reflective subject. That students must record their thoughts about what they've learned is also important — raising the awareness of the learner about his or her learning. Finally, the closing statement, which thanks students for their "help in improving curriculum and raising standards in FVP," puts the performances in the greater framework of the school, its curriculum, and its standards, acknowledging this as a community effort.

The idea of "Mouse Mobile" races as part of a Science Fair is certainly out of the ordinary, but it is not the only aspect of the Fulton Valley Prep project which makes this an excellent model for consideration when thinking about how to change our curriculum and assessment systems. The adaptation of existing models with local input added, the focus on student activity as central to the success of the work at hand, and the almost constant reflection on the learning process by students, all provide elements for thought by any who might want to move into these new areas of curriculum, instruction, and assessment. Borrowing a page from Fulton Valley Prep, you can reinvent your wheels by borrowing one or two of their tires!

SOCIAL STUDIES CURRICULUM AND PERFORMANCE ASSESSMENT

Social Studies as a discipline is plagued by the problem of content overload. While traditionally considered "History," Social Studies must also consider Economics, Anthropology, Archaeology, Sociology, Political Science, and Psychology as related disciplines, to name a few. But even if the focus were solely kept on History, there is still far too much content for students to genuinely learn — even if only studying the relatively brief period of American History! To consider engaging in *performance* assessments, then, Social Studies teachers have to judiciously limit their content goals. One way to help focus that limiting is to design courses around inquiry, and drive curriculum through questions.

Essential Questions are designed to go to the heart of a discipline — there is no right or wrong answer, only the creation of more questions which demand deeper study. They are questions which have relevancy to students. That is, they engage student curiosity. This doesn't mean they have to be *immediate* to the student's life, but are challenging in a way that demands a response because the question has a strength and relevance to all our lives. Essential questions cause students to ask more questions and directs their work as those questions emerge. They provoke "higher-order" thinking, demanding analysis, synthesis, and evaluation of problems — students *have to* go beyond simple fact-gathering and rote recall. Essential Questions, when well-designed, can be asked again and again throughout a course, a school year, across disciplines, and even throughout a student's career.

It is important to consider a concept like Essential Questions when working with a discipline like Social Studies because, all too often, the content of courses can overwhelm the intended focus of student learning. "Covering" material can easily replace genuine thinking and learning by students. But curriculum can be organized around far-ranging Essential Questions which develop more content-specific questions for focus. This interplay between the "big" questions, the interim/content questions, the materials used, and student *performance*, creates a curriculum and instruction design which departs from the traditional model. By its very nature, students will *have to become* active pursuers of solutions to questions. In the process, they will not only learn content, but also develop an array of skills — indeed, the repertoire Wiggins refers to — which they will use long after the course is over.

The following pages represent several Social Studies *performance assessments* which are intended to "cover" certain content areas, but are driven by questions, and not simply aimed at making sure students are "exposed" to the facts of history.

A "REVOLUTIONARY" PERFORMANCE TASK

Heathwood Hall Episcopal School in Columbia, South Carolina, provides a fine example of how students can pursue essential questions while still learning about important content outcomes. The focus on student-active, student-constructed **products** and *performances* creates the point of departure from traditional study of the French Revolution. Additionally, we see a conscious efforts by the teaching team to promote **habits** of sound learning in their students.

Heathwood Hall Episcopal School's 10th grade Humanities class uses a performance approach to studying the French Revolution. The assignment calls for teams of students to create a pamphlet (Fig. 2.3), with strict parameters as to structure, but freedom for student choice. Notable in this *performance* is its connection to the broader outcomes for the Humanities course and its connection to the Essential Questions which drive the course.

(Text continues on page 52.)

FIGURE 2.3: HEATHWOOD HALL — HUMANITIES 10

Course Name: **Humanities 10**

Grade Level: Tenth

Teachers: Ted Graf, Marshall James, Dan Palma

Skills to be taught or reinforced:

        Persuasive, analytical and "creative" writing
        The writing process (Multiple drafts and peer editing)
        usage in the context of their own papers and stories
        journal writing
        vocabulary development
        annotating and analytical reading
        interpreting literature
        preparing and rehearsing for presentations
        speaking and presenting in front of groups
        seminar participation and discussion
        How to extract and use research information from peridocials, books and other sources
        How to use a library and its variety of services
        How to determine a useful source

Habits to be encouraged:

        To be able to discern bias in writing and discussions
        To cooperate and recognize that the students can learn from each other
        To be able to defend a set of ideas ("thinking on one's feet")
        To listen to each other and tolerate a myriad of viewpoints
        To question sources, teachers and each other (Why does this matter?)

The Body of Knowledge:

        The Scientific Revolution (Hamlet)
        The Reformation (A Man for All Seasons)
        The French Revolution (A Tale of Two Cities, Danton)
        The Industrial Revolution (Jane Eyre, Frankenstein, Tess of the D'Urbervilles)
        The Russian Revolution (Dr. Zhivago)
        The Rise of the the Third Reich (Night)
        Post World War II (Lord of the Flies)

Essential Questions:

        Do revolutions improve society?
            What is a revolution?
            What forms do revolutions take?
            How do revolutions occur?
            Why do revolutions occur?

Humanities 10 -- News/Pamphlets for French Revolution
Mr. Graf, Mr. James, Mr. Palma

The Task

Each class will be divided into pamphlet groups of four members (these groups
may be logical outgrowths of your study buddies). Your task is to write and
assemble a newspaper or pamphlet from a period of time during the French
Revolution, as designated by your teacher. You must work with a team.
Separatists are not allowed on this project.
    The periods of time follow:

    a. May & June 1789
    b. July - October 1789
    c. 1791-1792
    d. 1793
    e. 1794 (may need a little extra research)

Your pamphlet must reflect a point of view. Your choices for that are either
the First, Second or Third Estate. Please follow syllabus for due dates.

Grading Criteria for Articles

Each student will write one "hard news" article and one "soft news" article.
For each of these pieces you will receive your own grade.

A.) The hard news should give an on-the-scene account of a major event during
your time period of the French Revolution. Your hard news article will be
evaluated on historic accuracy, attention to historical detail and the
following items:

    *Answer who? what? where? and when? **in sentence number one.**
    *Thoroughly answer why? next.
    *Touch on possible ramifications or results.
    *Your writing should be detailed and on-the-scene, **though never
      first or second person.**
    *The article should reflect accurate reporting and careful research
    *We will evaluate articles based on accuracy, journalistic voice,
      thoroughness, and technical competence (grammar, spelling).

B.) Each student will also write a "soft news" article. This could range
from "Letters to the Editor" to "Travel in Austria," or "Lives of the Rich and
On-The-Run." Book reviews, fashion, Op-Ed Pages and **original** political
cartoons are other options. These articles will be evaluated on the following
criteria:

    *Creativity & Imagination
    *Answer who? what? where? and when? and why? at some point.
    *Reflect accurately on some aspect of life during the revolution
    *Reflect the lifestyles at that time

Grading Criteria for Pamphlet

You will also receive a separate "team grade" for the overall quality of your
pamphlet. Everyone on the team will receive the same grade for this. Each
class will be provided with in-class computer time.
A **distinctive** pamphlet will be word processed, will have few, if any,
typographical errors, will have appropriate and clear illustrations, will be
attractive (graphics & lay-out), will be well-organized and will be
understandable to someone not in Humanities 10. In other words, a stranger
could pick it up and make sense of it. This pamphlet will accurately reflect
your chosen point of view.

An **honors** pamphlet will be word processed, will have some typographical
errors, few (if any) illustrations and will be well-organized. The point of
view will be clear from the first page. Understanding of this pamphlet will
be depend on your knowledge of the French Revolution.

A **competent** pamphlet will not necessarily be word processed but will still
look like a newspaper in that the articles will be in columns, etc. It will
be neatly presented, attractive and may include appropriate illustrations.
This pamphlet may be inconsistent in conveying point of view. There will
probably be tape, staples and glue involved with this one.

A **marginal** pamphlet will be incomplete or disorganized. In other words, you
might submit a bunch of articles stapled to each other. Point of view will be
inconsistent and this one is likely to fall apart when someone picks it up.
Disregard for due dates is another characteristic of a marginal pamphlet.

Looking at the course outline which precedes the performance task, note that *skills* and *habits* are presented to the students *before* the "Body of Knowledge" is listed. The importance of this cannot be overstated. When considering the development of a *performance-based* curriculum, the content (the Body of Knowledge) cannot be allowed to overwhelm those skills and habits which students need to know and be able to do no matter what problem they may be faced with. Concluding with the Essential Questions, the teaching team has, in an extremely brief format, made a rigorous curriculum manageable from a 10th graders' point of view. The nine texts the course revolves around are challenging, and the Essential Questions provide a provocative jumping off point which can be returned to again and again as the texts are explored. More than that, the Essential Questions can cross disciplinary boundaries and students can begin to make their own connections to other courses, the nightly news, their own lives. By looking closely at the French Revolution task, allowing it to cast its shadow back upon the valued skills and habits outcomes, we can see how performance assessments can be developed if we are willing to sacrifice content for questions.

THE NATURAL FLOW OF OUTCOMES TO QUESTIONS TO TASK

The beauty of this assessment is its simplicity. The significance of it is its clear connection to the habits and skills outcomes for the course, and its relationship to the Essential Questions. Consider first what students must do, then what skills they will need, what habits will be fostered, and how all of that is neatly folded into the Body of Knowledge and Essential Questions.

By cross-referencing between "The Task" and the "Skills to be taught or reinforced," we can see that students will have to:

♦   Write persuasively using the writing process.

♦   Develop usage in context.

♦   Develop vocabulary skills.

♦   Interpret literature.

♦   Determine useful sources and use the library for research.

This is no fewer than eight of the "Skills" which are final outcomes for the course!

In the same fashion, looking to the "Habits" outcomes, we can see that all five outcomes in that domain would also be required. *A Tale of Two Cities* and *Danton* would be sources for this task, but to fulfill the assignment students will clearly have to use many other sources. Finally, consider how the Essential Questions relate to the task at hand: With the focus on a period during the French Revolution era, where the student publication must assume one of the Estate's points of view, imagine the variety of answers to, "How do revolutions occur?" and "Why do revolutions occur?" Imagine the debate surrounding, "Do revolutions improve society?" The richness of this assignment emerges only as we look at the larger scope of the intended outcomes for the students.

Once again, we also find a published criteria accompanying the assignment. At the risk of sounding redundant, this is a key ingredient to performance assessments, a distinguishing characteristic, and an attribute which sets them apart from too many "evaluations" students are presently subjected to. As with other criteria and rubrics we have seen, this one also gives students a clear picture of their goal. Yet it does so in a way that guides their work. It is *part of the teaching/learning process*, and that is another important aspect of these criteria. Once we move into the realm of *performance assessment* we cannot separate curriculum from instruction and evaluation. They are all of the same cloth and the integrated nature of those elements provides the power in the activity.

As with planning backwards itself, we could look at the entire *performance assessment* process as a "backwards" activity, given traditional curriculum→instruction→testing paradigms. In this case, the students are given the assessment **first** — the *performance task*. This provides the vehicle for curriculum — the French Revolution — which, in turn, directs the instruction — a student-centered activity, constructing knowledge, and using teachers as coaches. Arming the students with the guidelines, outcomes, and expectations **before** they begin their work, demands engagement and responsibility. Most significantly, the Heathwood Hall assignment clearly addresses the *stated outcomes* for the course.

A Challenge for the Reader: Consider the possibilities for other *performance-based* assignments which might accompany the rest of the texts in the "Body of Knowledge" list. Think about which "Habits" and "Skill" outcomes you might want to address. Focus on one of the "Body of Knowledge" areas *while considering the Essential Questions.* What kind of *performance task* might you design for students? What other materials and resources could you bring in to add depth to the assignment? Would you address the presentation skills that this assignment didn't? Would you focus on the Essential Questions which this assignment didn't?

REVISITING PERFORMANCES, REINFORCING SKILLS AND HABITS

A value of *performance* assessments is that they can be revisited to reinforce skills and habits which are important outcomes for students. Because students must actively show what they know, repeating a *performance* assessment in form, with different content, gives both the student and teacher feedback as to how much progress the student has made. If earlier *performances* are kept as part of a portfolio system, it is easy for a student to review an earlier piece of work with the latest *performance.*

Such was the case with the two assignments (Fig. 2.4) which follow. Both of these were given in a 9th grade Western Civilization course at Bronxville High School in New York. The course's "content," technically, was the Dawn of Man to the Renaissance. Needless to say, there are far too many facts in that span to consider presenting a chronological survey of the history.

The focus for the course developed around essential questions, which considered how Western Civilization contributed to the heritage of the United States, and, as important, what the qualities of a good or just society might be. Among the content outcomes, too, an understanding of geography was considered important, and the two *performance* assessments which follow were designed to engage the students in that area.

As with the Heathwood Hall assessment, first note the list of "Exit Outcomes" identified before examining the *performance* task. The "Skills & Habits" list, in particular, makes up a significant part of the assessment, which, while focusing on geography, requires students to make choices and judgments which delve far deeper into their understanding of history.

(Text continues on page 60.)

FIGURE 2.4: BRONXVILLE HIGH SCHOOL —
9TH GRADE WESTERN CIVILIZATION COURSE

Exit Outcomes
9th Grade
Bil Johnson

Skills & Habits
- Research
- Writing in a variety of modes
- Analytical reading
- Working cooperatively in a group setting
- Working independently
- Effective listening
- Ability to speak publicly
- Effective time management
- Organization of materials, readings, etc.
- Good study habits
- Effective questioning
- Group discussion

Content
- The G.R.E.A.S.E.S. analytical model (Government, Religion, Economics, Art/Architecture, Science/Technology, Education, Social/Cultural Values) to understand cultures over time and geographic locations
- The foundations of Western Civilization, using the analytical model. Understanding where "we" (United States) come from.
- Basic cause-and-effect --- the flow of history as logical & predictable (if you know how to look)
- Art/architecutre appreciation
- Knowing primary/secondary sources
- Current events

Attitudes / Behaviors
- Responsible
- Open-minded
- Fair-minded
- Courteous, respectful
- Curiosity
- Reflective

Essential Questions
- How did we (the U.S.) get here?
- What is a good society/civilization?
- What is a fair or just society?
- What is a good citizen?

Western Civ. Final Project, First quarter

Geography Challenge

You are an ace Travel Agent, the best in your Bureau but you don't always get along with your supervisor. Your boss has come to you with a unique problem. A team of archaeologists and anthropologists from all over the United States wants to take a trip in which they visit several museum in England, a few museums in France, the ruins of ancient Babylon, the pyramids and the sphinx in Egypt, and the Holy City of Jerusalem. They want to travel by plane, train, car, bus, and boat.

Your boss has made it quite clear that your job is on the line if you don't do the following:

#1. Arrange all the travel plans for the group, complete with MAPS, detailing the routes you recommend. They are all starting in New York.

#2. Explain, in writing, the step-by-step (or stop-by-stop) itinerary the group will follow. That is, **WHERE** they will go; **HOW** they will get there; **WHAT** they will do and see at each place when they are there.

The boss has also said you will get a **BONUS** (yes, that means Extra Credit) if you can come up with a price breakdown for the group, too. How much will each mode of transportation cost to go from one place to another? What's the price of hotels where they stay? How much should they expect to spend on meals?

Be prepared to make your presentation, using maps and your written itinerary, on Tuesday, November 12th in class.

Any questions?

Good luck. Have fun.

Assessment Criteria for First Quarter Final Project, Western Civilization

To get an **A** on the project you **MUST** do all of the following:
    1. Have complete and clear maps drawn and labeled.
    2. Have a complete itinerary written, clearly explaining the trip, step-by-step,
    including details of WHAT they will see that relates to them as
    anthropologist and archaeologists (that means, for example, **which** museums would they
    want to visit in England and France). It also means you would clearly
    explain **how** they would travel from one place to another (car, boat, plane, etc.),
    and how long they should expect to travel using that mode of transportation.
    3. Clearly present your final plan to the class using good public speaking style:
        clear diction, visual aids, good posture, a sense of seriousness.

To get a **B** on the project a student would:
    1. Have maps drawn and labeled, but not finely detailed.
    2. Have a written itinerary, explaining the trip step-by-step but not always
        clearly explaining the details.
    3. Present the final plan but not as clearly or directly as a good public speaker
        needs to be, using visual aids that are not as clear as they need to be.

To get a **C** on the project a student would:
    1. Have maps drawn but show little concern for detail and/or have things
        mis-labeled or unidentified.
    2. Have a written itinerary which was confusing and somewhat unclear about
        how they group is traveling, what order they are seeing things in, etc.
    3. Present the final plan but not speak up clearly and use weak visual aid support.

To get a **D** on the project a student would:
    1. Draw incomplete maps with sloppy or no labeling, reflecting a clear lack of concern
        for details.
    2. Write an itinerary which is confusing or missing information which would be
        necessary for the travellers.
    3. Present the final plan in a casual and "unprofessional" way.
    4. Only do two of the three requirements.

To **FAIL** this project a student would:
    1. Do little or no mapwork.
    2. Do little or no written work.
    3. Fail to present a final plan to the class.

Western Civilization
ART & REFORMATION
Live Tour!

Because of the exceptional job you did last fall planning the itinerary for the Archaeologists interested in touring the Ancient World, you have been given another assignment from the A204 Travel Agency!

This time you have a more challenging problem: the group is a combination of clergy-people and student-artists. They do have ONE interest in common: they all LOVE the Renaissance. Each group, in fact, has submitted a list of the people of the Renaissance whose hometowns or work-towns or parishes they want to visit.

Your challenge, then, is to design a tour (complete with *detailed* maps) which makes everyone in the group happy. They expect to see a presentation of maps, with explanations of what they will see where starting on May 21st (Thursday).

Here's the list of Renaissance people they want to "visit."

Reformation Figures/Humanists	Artists
Erasmus	Donatello
Machiavelli	Jan Van Eyck
Thomas More	Albrecht Durer
Martin Luther	Botticelli
Henry VIII	Alberti
Zwingli	Raphael
John Calvin	Leonardo da Vinci
Shakespeare	Michelangelo
	Titian
	Hans Holbein
	Pieter Breugel
	Hieronymus Bosch

You may direct the tour to visit the works of a famous artist (which may not be in the artist's "hometown") and the sites of famous historical events (where a reformer or humanist did something significant) so they also get a real "tour" of Europe as they get to see what they have gone there for.

<u>Criteria: Renaissance Tour</u>

<u>A:</u> 1. A clear, detailed map, precisely showing each place which will be visited during the tour.

2. A well- written explanation of the map which explains WHY each stop was chose & WHAT the historical significance of the stop is. There should be some explanation of why the trip's itinerary is logical -- why it makes sense to go from this place to the next, etc.

3. A clear, articulate oral presentation explaining the trip, fielding questions with responsive, articulate answers.

<u>B:</u> 1. A fairly clear, fairly detailed map indicating where the tour will go, but lacking precise details or clarity in parts.

2. A written explanation of the map which explains WHY the stops were chosen but doesn't go into depth about the historical significance of the stop. It briefly explains the logic behind the trip's planning but doesn't connect the stops in a well-explained fashion.

3. A clear, fairly articulate presentation of the trip which answers <u>most</u> questions intelligently and accurately.

<u>C:</u> 1. A map presents the tour, and each place visited, but is not highly detailed or precise. It would not be immediately clear to someone what the purpose of the map was.

2. A written explanation of the tour which tells WHERE each stop is and gives a brief reason as to WHY the stop is being made but lacks any significant historical detail.

3. An oral presentation superficially explains the stops of the tour without elaboration and questions are not fully or clearly answered.

<u>D:</u> 1. A map is drawn with indications of where the tour might stop. Minimal effort has been made; minimal results are shown.

2. A written explanation of the map is equally sketchy and minimal in its effort and results.

3. Oral presentation reveals that the map and writing author have not fully researched the topic and are not in command of the assignment.

<u>E:</u> Work is not turned in by deadline and/or is of such poor quality as to not be recognizable in relation to the assignment given.

Note that the second assessment refers to the first, and that the dates indicate there is a 6-month gap between the two. Revisiting the format of a *performance* assessment proves a very effective means for not only reinforcing valued skills and outcomes, but also evaluating how well the assessment itself works.

While geography was a small component of this course, it provided a vehicle for students to *apply* knowledge about people, places, and events in a context which was "authentic" and fun. As with so many performance assessments, this one is predicated on the concept of *knowledge-in-use*, and its basic design grows from committment to that concept.

In looking at the assessments, the Reader is once again encouraged to cross-reference between the listed Exit Outcomes (what the students should know and be able to do by June) and the *performance* assignment. The confluence of curriculum→instruction→ assessment should once again become apparent.

REPEATING A FORMAT, INCREASING THE CHALLENGE

The striking difference between these two assessments is the level of complexity called for in the second one. While the first "Travel Agent" assignment is basically a mapping project with specific parameters, the second requires the application of far more content knowledge. Both, of course, take several very traditional curricular goals — geography and the study of ancient civilizations — but casts them in a new fashion requiring students to actively present what they know.

Once again, if we examine the "Skills & Habits," we can identify *at least eight* from the list. And, while not *directly* addressing the Essential Questions, it requires little imagination to see how simple, given the content, any number of connections to those questions could be made. In deciding *what* their tourists will see, students will implicitly be making judgments about what a "good" society or civilization is — and follow-up discussions will very explicitly address those issues. Through the investigation of the humanists and artists in the second assignment, students will have to construct their own views about values in the Renaissance, and the ensuing discussions will raise the issue about what a "fair" or "just" society is. Ultimately, comparisons to our present world will be made, too, in an effort to see if knowledge gained about an historical era can, indeed, be transferred to profit the present.

The **presentation** requirement in both assignments shows how students can be given tasks which they can compare over time, creating the opportunity for self-assessment. This also directly addresses a set of skills which most schools *claim* as important outcomes — speaking and listening — but actually asks students to *perform* those skills. Too often skills such as these are listed as "goals for graduates" without any serious or methodical attempt at insuring that students actually leave school with them. How many schools or districts have *evidence* that their students can, in fact, adequately present themselves as public speakers? How do we make sure students have, in fact, become effective listeners? To simply *tell* students to "listen carefully" or "speak up" is not enough. We must build into the curriculum→instruction→assessment system opportunities for students to engage in these skills again and again, subjecting themselves to critical scrutiny. This is not an easy task, but it is crucial if we are to graduate students *knowing* they have developed specific skills *throughout* their career.

Again, the need for published criteria and standards, as well as scoring rubrics, are a crucial aspect of accountability — for students **and** teachers. In both of these examples, students received an "Assessment Criteria" *with* the assignment, clearly announcing what the expectations were. And, while these are somewhat flawed rubrics, they are far better than the usual expectation — a teacher's exhortation to "work hard and do a good job." And, again, a scoring rubric creates two important opportunities for students which are seldom available — a format for self-assessment and a platform for discussion *with the teacher* about "why" the performance was rated as it was.

The creation of opportunities for dialogue about the teaching/learning process is another significant feature of performance assessments and the characteristic which clearly distinguishes them from many student evaluations which presently exist. Consider what happens with most assessments students engage in. They receive a grade with, at best, some comments from the teacher. If it is a standardized test which is not locally developed, students never even know *which* questions they got right or wrong! But even when they receive written feedback on an essay, for example, the remarks are cryptic and leave little room for dialogue. Part of this, of course, has to do with the fact that teachers have far too many papers (or even tests) to grade at once, not allowing them the chance to write extensive commentary for students. This raises another issue worth considering, and speaks to the design of assessments such as these geography tasks — that is, repeating the form of an assignment so that students can gauge their own progress.

PERFORMANCE ASSESSMENTS: WHAT DO WE KNOW?

In summary, then, what do we know about *Performance Assessment*?

- ◆ Performance assessments are the basic building block of a new assessment system.

- ◆ Performance assessments clarify valued outcomes by asking students to actually *enact* those outcomes, thereby presenting evidence that students have achieved those outcomes.

- ◆ Performance assessments provide opportunities for students to become self-assessors and create an avenue for student/teacher dialogue about student performance and progress.

- ◆ Performance assessments create a platform for teachers to assess the progress of their own work: Can we *see* student progress toward valued outcomes?

- ◆ Performance assessments require "front-loaded" work, starting with a focus on outcomes and working *backwards* to create appropriate tasks for students. The very nature of classroom work by teachers is changed by a performance assessment system.

- ◆ Performance assessments create a very public account-ability system.

- ◆ Performance assessments change the nature of the cur-riculum→instruction→evaluation paradigm by embed-ding each angle of that system *with* the added com-ponent of student engagement, requiring a far more integrated approach to teaching and learning.

♦ Performance assessments provide critical lenses for examining our basic system of teaching and learning, calling into question age-old practices (everyone must progress uniformly, grading is a mystery to students, etc.) and requiring a reassessment of all we do in school.

Starting a performance assessment system is a tall order, no doubt, and a road filled with potholes and obstacles, but the potential rewards for students and teachers are great, indeed. What we have seen here is that individual teachers can embark on that road without leaving their current practice altogether and forever. In fact, it would be recommended that a teacher, or team of teachers, or even a faculty, consider implementing such a system incrementally — but with *committment*. No one will "get it right" the first time. What teachers learn is as important as what students learn in this system, and, even if the initial designs are not earth-shattering or brilliant, they will be no worse, certainly, than the system which now exists. If only because the teaching/learning process is *opened up* to the students and a move toward greater public accountability is established, this system will reap immediate benefits. It requires certain courage and commitment from those practitioners willing to implement it. But paths have already been established, as this chapter illustrates. The "wheel" need not be reinvented; it only has to be fitted to your vehicle.

3

EXHIBITIONS:
SHOW WHAT YOU KNOW
— FOR HIGH STAKES

Exhibitions have been referred to throughout the first half of this book. The idea of **Exhibition** has been popularized by the Coalition of Essential Schools, and owes its present notoriety to Theodore Sizer, chairman of that organization.

First in *Horace's Compromise* (1984), and then again in *Horace's School* (1992), Sizer proposed that American schools restructure themselves in such a way that students would have to meet certain *performance* standards for graduation. According to the sixth "Common Principle" of the Coalition,

> The diploma should be awarded on a successful final demonstration of mastery for graduation — an Exhibition. This Exhibition by the student of his or her grasp of the

central skills and knowledge of the school's program may
be jointly administered by the faculty and higher authorities.

Horace's School, p. 208

Having presented the concept of the Exhibition in 1984, Sizer
provides "sample" Exhibitions throughout his 1992 text. By that
time, numerous schools had embarked down the road to Exhibitions,
and examples from some of those schools appear in this chapter.
Before examining those examples, however, a more thorough explanation of Exhibitions is necessary.

Because the Coalition of Essential Schools does not promote
a cookie-cutter approach to school philosophy, Exhibitions will necessarily differ from school to school. Nonetheless, there will be some
basic similarities, and their commonality stems from Sizer's basic
ideas. Examining his conception of *Exhibitions* provides clear guidelines for our own understanding of these assessments.

Sizer, in his appreciation of America's educational history, heark-
ens back to the 19th century idea of *public exhibitions* which marked
the end of the school year in many small towns. In a festive atmosphere, the townsfolk would turn out to hear students recite and
cipher — a low-key public accountability and a presentation of what
their property tax was paying for. Owing the form to that tradition,
today's Exhibitions are also designed for public accountability, but
in a far more high-stakes fashion. As Sizer notes,

Why an *Exhibition*? The word clearly states its purpose:
the student must Exhibit the products of his learning. If he
does well, he can convince himself that he can use knowledge
and he can so convince others. It is the academic equivalent
of being able to sink free throws. . . . To shoot baskets well
one needs to practice. Going to school is practicing to use
one's mind well. . . . However, the heart of it is in the play.
Merely "knowing" ideas is as inert as knowing that one
has to sink the free throw from the foul line. One has to
actually sink the shot, has to *use* the ideas, has to be in the
habit of using them, and *use* is always far more complicated
than simple recall of propositions or rules or even an analysis
of them.

Horace's School, pp. 25–26

The key to Exhibitions, then, involves the application of what students have learned — *knowledge-in-use*. Sizer makes it clear in his descriptions and sample Exhibitions that these are intended to be rigorous challenges, worthy of earning a diploma. Many are multidisciplinary tasks, requiring students to apply knowledge and skills across a variety of fields. And, as has been noted earlier, these Exhibitions have an impact on the entire curriculum. Again, as Sizer explains:

> The Exhibition, then, is not only the target. It is also a representation of the way one prepares to reach the target. That is, school is about practicing to wrap one's mind around real and complex ideas, those of fundamental consequence for oneself and for the culture. It is not merely about "coverage," or being informed, or displaying skills. It is the demonstration of the employment of all of these toward important and legitimate ends.
>
> The final Exhibition is a "test," yes; but it is really an affirmation for the student herself and for her larger community that what she has long practiced in school, what skills and habits she has developed, have paid off.
>
> *Horace's School*, p. 26

As described earlier, *performance assessments* are the stepping stones toward Exhibitions. And that speaks to the concept of creating a performance assessment *system*. Because performance assessments are embedded in curriculum and instruction, they cannot be implemented in a simple "substitution" fashion — trading a *performance* for a quiz or test, for example. Looking at a fully developed assessment system, we can begin to see that it presents curriculum and assessment designers with an array of possibilities — which all grow logically and organically from a simple design plan.

The key to designing Exhibitions or *performance assessments* is clearly knowing what it is our students should know and be able to do. And that means in quite specific terms. As has been noted before, all too often the "outcomes" developed by teachers, faculties, and school districts are simple statements of the broad skills, areas of knowledge, and basic behavioral dispositions it is *hoped* students will graduate with. So, it is not unusual for an "outcome statement" for Any School USA to read:

♦ Students will demonstrate critical thinking skills specifically applied to problems in American History.

♦ Students will be problemsolvers in mathematics, applying concepts from Algebra and Geometry.

♦ Students will demonstrate proficiency in writing across a variety of genres in Language Arts.

♦ Students will demonstrate critical thinking, problem-solving skills in several areas of the Sciences, including Biology and Chemistry.

These are wonderful statements, of course, which prove totally meaningless when we consider their implications for curriculum and instruction. Which "critical thinking skills" and what "problems in American History?" What kinds of "problemsolving in mathematics?" Questions like these can be asked of most "outcome statements" which have been developed by schools over the past 5–7 years.

The commitment to requiring students to *exhibit* what they have learned, however, brings about dramatic changes in curriculum and instruction. And the starting point toward that commitment is greater clarity in outcome statements. Because standardized tests, and even schoolwide or teacher-developed tests, often only ask for lower-order thinking — recall and comprehension of simple facts and algorithms, and only the most basic application of those ideas — students are seldom held accountable for truly demonstrating what they know and are able to do. In more clearly defining the "critical-thinking" or "problemsolving" we expect from our students, we begin to tackle the issues of curriculum and instruction from new directions, with new perspectives.

Several aspects of Exhibitions should be noted in the examples which follow. Identifying specific outcomes expected of students should be apparent. In many of the examples, criteria and rubrics are given to the students, clarifying expectations and making outcomes known. In all the examples, the explanation of the project, the procedures expected, and many of the skills required, are also noted for the students *at the beginning* of the assignment. Equally important to consider is the shadow cast backward from these Exhibitions. That is, if these are *milepost* performances for students, what would the *checkpoints* have been along the way? This is significant to note because that examination, more than any other, guides the development of curriculum and instruction design.

With each of the examples presented, we will analyze the Exhibition with an eye toward *what was expected of students* **along the way?** This should provide clues and guideposts for curriculum and instruction development.

The first example presented is from an individual teacher who has embarked on his own road to Exhibitions. Working within a "traditional" curricular framework, there has been a commitment to see students more completely *exhibit* their learning through a multitask assignment. This Exhibition has replaced a "final exam" and, as you will see, the tasks create serious challenges for students.

TRADITIONAL CURRICULUM, PERFORMANCE ASSESSMENTS

Alan Levin teaches Physics at Columbia High School in South Orange-Maplewood, New Jersey. In many ways, the Physics course may not have seemed different from others given across the country, until the 1993–94 school year, when Alan decided to depart from the traditional final exam and present his students with a final Exhibition. Examining this performance assessment reveals many of the principles previously discussed — increased student responsibility and ownership of the tasks, knowledge-in-use, and a direct focus on higher-order thinking skills. Most significantly, it is presented to the students with a *clear rationale* for **why** this Exhibition is replacing the more traditional test. In doing so, Alan presents a fine argument for the "both/and" approach, being careful not to cast his Exhibition into an either/or frame *against* multiple-choice testing. As previously mentioned, assessments should be designed to provide feedback about student learning — there is no *one way* to do them and there is no one **right** way either. Alan's rationale makes that point to his students, explaining why he believes this Exhibition will be more useful to them at this time.

Another important point to note is that the Exhibition is spread out over several days — students are not expected to "cram" for the test. On the contrary, what is valued, particularly on Part I, is thoughtful and reflective use of knowledge learned in the course. Because of the design of the problem, there is no concern about cheating. In fact, one of the most appealing elements of performance assessments and Exhibitions is that they can't be "cheated" on because each student will have to devise his or her own solution to the problems at hand. Let's examine the Exhibition and then analyze it for outcomes, checkpoints, and effectiveness.

TURNING TRADITIONAL CURRICULUM INTO EXHIBITIONS

By looking at each phase of this Exhibition (Fig. 3.1, beginning on p. 72), we can see how a teacher can move from the realm of traditional testing to more authentic assessment of students. The introduction to the "Final Exam" presents students with a clear rationale as to why they are moving to a new type of assessment. By reading the first few paragraphs carefully we can see how this assessment will be an improvement over "sixty odd multiple choice questions." And, while arguments are presented to the students explaining how that type of test could be used for feedback, the final introductory paragraph makes a strong case for the Exhibition: students will have to "think and create, . . . evaluate, synthesize, and 'think physics.'" And here we have an outcome statement for higher-order thinking skills, as well as a note as to how students will have choices — "a large part of the questions are of your own design." These elements distinguish this Exhibition from a traditional final exam on a number of important levels. Looking carefully at each segment of the Exhibition further illuminates how this assessment challenges students to "show what they know."

Part I of this Exhibition is clearly for high stakes — it counts for 50% of the student's grade. Significantly, though, the responsibility is placed on the student to determine what was important in the course — and to *apply* those concepts to the real world. We can easily see how this is a radical departure from a traditional teacher-designed, multiple-choice test. Students determine "major topics and concepts in physics" and then "create and solve problems" with data they collect in the "real world." The assignment notes that students must carefully document their choices with evidence ("include not only mathematical work ups but a careful explanation") and must represent their work in pictures and graphics, too. The "Challenge" to present examples of multiple physics concepts in one or two examples or situations provides the platform for students to exhibit the higher-order thinking skill of synthesis, truly showing what they know.

Many science courses use Amusement Parks as real world examples of scientific concepts in action, and this course was no exception. However, this is a fine example of using the year's Amusement Park project as a *checkpoint* on the way to the *milepost*. Part II — "You Can't Break the Laws of Physics" presents students with a highly challenging problem, which requires the **application** of what they have learned, **and** then asks them to elaborate on that knowledge. This is an "in-class" assignment but, significantly, the students have been given the problem beforehand, so they can think, reflect, experiment, and delve into what it is they may know or not know about physics. And even if students consulted with each other before the in-class problem was presented, every student still has to create his or her own solutions and design changes! As with so many performance assessments, if we examine this problem, it becomes apparent that the expectations for students is well beyond the simple regurgitation of formulae or algorithms — it *demands* that students pick out and explain those formulae and algorithms in ways that clearly relate to the problem at hand.

Similarly, Part III takes an everyday occurrence, brewing a pot of coffee, and presents a problem which "can be answered in a simple way or with more complexity." The challenge, it appears, is to present the complexity — how much *does* a cup of coffee cost? Again, "classic" Physics topics are involved — mechanical, heat, and electrical energy — but, again, they are presented in a nonroutine and challenging format. And, as with the Ultra Coaster problem, students will have to perform during a class period on a designated time and day. As we consider what the problem is asking students to do, the complexity of the task emerges: What do students have to know about various forms of energy? How must they know how to apply abstract concepts about energy to the very practical problem of cost? How many calculations and possibilities can arise in solving this problem? Here, we see, in a wonderfully rich example, what a "problemsolving" outcome *really* looks like. It is easy to list "problemsolving" as a district's goal for its students: it is far more impressive to actually *see* the kind of challenging problem students will be faced with.

(Text continues on page 77.)

FIGURE 3.1: COLUMBIA HIGH SCHOOL — PHYSICS ASSESSMENT

1993-1994 Physics Assessment -- Final Exam

This year's final exam represents a radical change from those of past years. The usual exam consists of sixty odd multiple choice questions that the teacher has distilled from 180 days of course work. The score on this test represents what?

    a. How well the student understands the "pieces" of physics.
    b. The guessing ability of some.
    c. The quickness of others to complete 5 dozen questions in 90 minutes.
    d. None of the above.
    e. _____

In fact, the old exam for all its problems did have some real value. It asks that students review a full year of physics, an important activity. The physics teachers created a test that asked something about almost all aspects of the course. After grading, the department could use the results to determine on average how well different students and groups of students compared, both within and between classes over time. It was even helpful (in theory) in determining which aspects of the class needed further examination. Finally, since some final exams needed to be given last multiple choice lent themselves to that criteria.

So, what's wrong? Actually nothing, this new assessment hopes to do better. The new version of the Great Adventure Lab represented the difference between "plug and chug" and think and create. This series of exercises also is designed to force you to evaluate, synthesize, and "think physics." There are no trick questions, a large part the questions are of your own design. The assessment comes in three parts:

Part I - The Physics of _____

The normal way that students review for final exams is to start at the beginning of the course and determine what is important, review the major concepts, recall the formulas and practice examples of the types of problems those concepts and formulas represented. Your assignment is to do just that. First determine what are major topics and concepts in physics. Next find examples of those concepts in the "real" world. Gather data (real or semi-fictional) and create and solve some problems with that data. Your report should include not only the mathematical work ups but a careful explanation of how your example demonstrates the concept. Pictures and graphics are essential.

A Challenge - Since many examples or situations may contain multiple concepts more credit will be given to examples that interweave as many as possible. The only one that you can't use is the Physics of Amusement Parks. The possibilities are endless from The Physics of My House to . . . .

This assignment is due on Monday, June 20, 1994 at the end of class. It will count 50% of your final exam grade. If it is not turned in that day you will get a zero for this part of the exam. Not coming to school will not excuse you from the due date. If you wake up that morning and are too sick to come to school (or what ever excuse you have) call me and I will personally pick it up from your house. This is no joke and my deadline is absolute!

Part II - You Can't Break the Laws of Physics . . .

The Great Adventure Amusement Park has installed a new ride for the 1995 season. They have engaged the engineering firm of Dewy, Cheatum and Howe to check out the ride for safety. You have been brought in for a second opinion. Your job will be, given the engineering specifications, to evaluate the ride's features and double check the report prepared by Dewy, Cheatum and Howe.

This part of the assessment will be done in class on Friday June 17, 1994. It will count 25% of your final exam grade.

Part III - . . . but you can take a coffee break

This part of the evaluation will be no surprise to those of you with good memories and parents to those who came to the open house in December. The question is "What does it cost to make a cup of coffee?" The heart of this question relates the concepts of energy in several forms. Mechanical, heat and electrical. It can be answered in a simple way or with more complexity. Your challenge is to bring some complexity to the problem. I will bring in an actual coffee pot to perform the brewing and will supply data about it. You should do some outside research and bring in data that you feel will be useful (or essential).

This part of the assessment will be completed in class on Monday June 20, 1994. It will count 25% of your exam grade.

The Ultra Coaster

The Great Adventure Amusement Park has installed a new ride for the 1995 season. The Ultra Coaster was designed to provide a ride of maximum thrills while at the same time transport passengers from one side of the park to the other. (The return of the coaster is underground and is not shown on the diagram.) The engineering firm of Dewy, Cheatum and Howe has just certified the ride. They say that the ride will work as designed (see design specifications below) and will be safe. Your job is to further certify the ride or make recommendations for modification based upon problems you find in during your analysis.

Technical Specifications

Maximum mass of the coaster fully loaded   1,000 kg
Maximum velocity not to exceed 40 m/sec
Maximum g force not to exceed 4 g's

The specifications below can be modified if necessary

Maximum braking force   5,000 N
The ride will use 20,000 watt electrical motors to raise the cars to the top of the first hill in 40 sec.
Height of first hill   100m
Radius at top of loop   10m
Radius at bottom of loop   30m
Radius of cork screw   20m
Braking section   120m

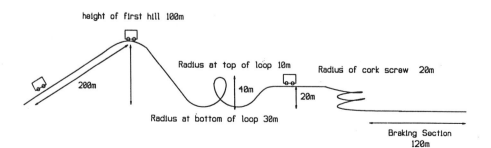

Physics Assessment Part II
You Can't Break the Laws of Physics

The Ultra Coaster
Summary Page

Problems With Design	Problem Solution Design Changes

Physics Assessment Part III
Time for a coffee break

What does it cost to make a cup of coffee?

The coffee pot that I will be using today was given to me as a gift from Mr. Cohen more than 10 years ago when he shared the back office. The last one I had blew up and I have no idea what make it was. The current pot has make over 5000 cups of coffee and rather than have some fancy German label is a good old Mr. Coffee Machine. The machine is completely devoid of sophistication and simply heats water from tap temperature to 100°C and pours this water over the coffee grounds allowing the rich full bodied taste to drip into the waiting pot below. Your job is to determine the cost of a cup of coffee. The heart of this question relates the concepts of energy in several forms. Mechanical, heat and electrical. It can be answered in a simple way or with more complexity. The facts that I will supply at this time are the starting temperature of the tap water and the wattage of the Mr. Coffee Machine. Make sure your work is shown in a clear way and organized format, indicating the assumptions you have used in your solutions.

A MIDDLE SCHOOL HUMANITIES EXHIBITION

Hibberd Middle School in Richmond, Indiana, implemented an interdisciplinary Humanities program in the early 1990s. An integral part of that program has been the development of a performance assessment system which teachers have articulated in a written statement. Guided by that philosophical statement, the staff has worked at developing an assessment system which will measure student growth, develop students' abilities to self-assess, and serve as a gauge of program effectiveness for teachers.

As a member of the Coalition of Essential Schools, the curriculum at Hibberd is guided by a "less is more" philosophy and driven by Essential Questions. The Exhibition presented here (Fig. 3.2) is designed for 8th graders, addresses a series of Essential Questions, features both group and individual work, and includes rubrics intended for group, individual, self-, and peer evaluation. The outcomes for this Exhibition are not stated the way Alan Levin's were in the Physics Exhibition, but are embedded in the assignment. A task for the Reader, then, is to identify what *outcomes* — skills, knowledge, and dispositions — are expected of students in this Exhibition.

One other note of importance here: Read the *Assessment for Humanities* statement carefully and note its references. This Humanities team (led by Randy Wisehart and Tammy Rhoades) clearly invested a great deal of time and thought into their efforts. They are philosophically grounded in their approach and carefully considered the directions they wish to head in. And, while the statement and the Exhibition may not be "perfect," they are both significant advances for students, parents, and teachers as we strive for greater clarity in our work.

ESSENTIAL QUESTIONS, OUTCOMES, AND SHOWING WHAT YOU KNOW

After reading the Assessment statement by the Humanities team, it is clear that the Hibberd program has made a serious commitment to performance assessment. While still having to give "letter grades," the teachers have clearly articulated *where* those grades will come from and have made student self-assessment a primary goal of their

(Text continues on page 83.)

FIGURE 3.2: HIBBERD MIDDLE SCHOOL –
ASSESSMENT FOR HUMANITIES

ASSESSMENT FOR HUMANITIES

(adapted from Paulson 1991, Wiggins 1987,
Wiggins 1991, Coalition of Essential Schools
1990, Coalition of Essential Schools 1990)

The aim of assessment is to impove student performance as students show what they know and are able to do as opposed to dealing solely with memorization of facts. Assessment is an ongoing process whether done by teachers, by students assessing the work of peers, or students doing self-assessment. Assessment must be timely and frequent. It does not measure, but helps improve, gives models, provides opportunities for feedback, and allows opportunities for successive approximation. As students continually strive to make progress toward high standards, teachers must point out to students to what extent they are progressing toward the exemplars (i.e. examples of high standards) until students internalize what high standards really are. High standards are to be found in completed tasks, products, and performances that require such intellectual virtues as craftmanship, self-criticism, and persistence. Assessment at an ongoing informal level will consist of brief teacher-student conferences, processing out of group activities, and continual processing of daily workshop activities. Formal assessment will involve discussion\critiquing of individual goals during goal conferences, evaluation of humanities portfolios, and critiquing of culminating exhibitions.

Although letter grades will be assigned to students, those grades will be determined by a combination of teacher and student evaluation and collaboration. The grades for individual students will be determined by goals conferences between the teacher and individual student, oral presentations, participation in group work, exhibitions\presentations, daily assignments, and portfolios of student work.

The oral presentations, participation in group work, and daily assignments will be assessed in a variety of ways including teacher evaluation, self-evaluation, and peer evaluation. The exhibitions\presentations will be assessed by teacher\student critiquing, i.e. to what extent did the exhibition\presentation approximate the examples of excellence already demonstrated and discussed. The goals conference will consist of the student and teacher formally setting up an appointment to discuss the extent to which the student has accomplished goals previously agreed upon by the teacher and student. The portfolio will be assessed as a part of the goals conference. In the seventh grade it will include a persuasive essay (and in the eighth grade a compare\contrast essay) and other finished drafts of writing and creative projects, including but not limited to samples of art work that enhances understanding of key concepts, musical applications of critical thinking, and video tapes of plays, interviews, role playing, etc.

ESSENTIAL QUESTION PROJECT SPRING 1994
WHO BUILT AMERICA?
HOW HAVE WOMEN AND MINORITIES HELPED BUILD AMERICA?
HOW WILL YOU CONTINUE TO SHAPE AMERICA?

There will be two components to your final project. First, you will collaborate with two or three classmates on a group project. Next, you will write a personal reflection on the Essential Question. The group part should be completed by Friday, May 6th. Presentations of group projects will be during the week of May 9-13. We will assign presentation times.The individual part is due no later than Friday, May 13th. (No points off for turning them in early!)

In your groups of 3 or 4 students, you must produce a talk show, debate, or trial based on the Essential Question. You must include historical figures that reflect different time periods and diverse backgrounds. You must also include at least one fictional character to take part in the presentation.

You must include the following in the group presentation:

    -at least one fictional character (perhaps to moderate the talk show or judge the trial.

    -at least four historical figures as guests or witnesses. At least two must be from after 1900. The other two may be from any period in American history.

    -a bibliography of sources your group has consulted.

    -an outline or written script of your presentation.

    -visual aids (posters, costumes, props....

For your group projects, if you are planning a talk show or debate, make sure you plan both good questions for the historical guests and good responses for them to answer with. Don't just wing it on the day of your presentation. If you are planning a trial, make sure you plan how to tie it to the Essential Question. You could put someone on trial for standing up for what they believe and have some historical witnesses testify to what they believe - Why they support this defendant or why they don't support her.

Plan for your presentations to be about 15 minutes long. We will once again use a self evaluation and peer evaluations for the presentations.

This is your task for your **individual** part.

It is the year 2070. You've had a long life. A very long life. Who from American history has really influenced you? What kind of people have really built America, in your opinion? Have you been influenced by both men and women? by people of different races and backgrounds? What did you do in your life that reflects the influence of people from American history? Write a letter (perhaps to your great grandchildren or perhaps to Ms. Rhoades who has been frozen and is soon due to be thawed out...)

You must include:

-references to at least two historical figures. At least one must be from the 20th century.

-a well-written letter in **final draft form** of two to three pages. (Extensions will be given only to people who want to write a lot more than two or three pages, not to people who are just lazy.)

-references to what you have specifically done with your life and how you were influenced. You can include books you read way back in 1994, important people in your life, important things you did if they seem appropriate.

-specific things you did as an adult (your career or careers, your education...)

-references to the personal qualities of people in American history that you admire or have been influenced by.

Do not wait until the last minute to begin. Plan to use the half hour of reading time at home to read, write, or research for this project.

GROUP PROJECT ASSESSMENT RUBRIC

name

1. Interesting opening easy to hear. Flows well, few stops and starts.	10	8	7	6	5	Beginning not interesting Several stops and starts
2. Characters clearly explain how they shaped America with specific examples.	10	8	7	6	5	It is not clear how the characters shaped America Few examples
3. Questions help characters explore who shaped America. Back and forth questions and answers. Characters talk to each other.	10	8	7	6	5	Superficial questions and answers. Answers don't fit questions Characters just read separate scripts and don't talk to each other.
4. Creative and interesting. Use visuals or props or interesting dialogue.	10	8	7	6	5	Not at all interesting. No visuals or props. Parts just read. Sounds like separate reports.
5. Bibliography complete with at least 4 sources.	5	4	3	2	1	Bibliography missing
6. Outline or draft used. Group was clearly prepared.	5	4	3	2	1	Group winged it. Clearly not prepared.

Self-evaluation

1. I used my time well	5	4	3	2	1	I wasted lots of time.
2. I did my share.	5	4	3	2	1	Others did my work.

INDIVIDUAL ESSENTIAL PROJECT RUBRIC 1994

_____
name

	10	8	7	6	5	
1. Several specific examples from history to support an opinion on the essential question. It is very clear why the student has chosen these specific people.	10	8	7	6	5	Few if any examples from history. Example does not seem to support an opinion. It is not clear why these people were chosen.
2. Interesting and/or creative. The writer of the letter seems to be a real person with a distinct voice. Clear opinions are expressed. Examples from a future life clearly show how a person was affected by significant Americans.	10	8	7	6	5	Not interesting. Few, if any examples from what writer did in her future life No voice. Writer does not seem like a real person.
3. In final draft form. Few, if any, errors in spelling, punctuation or mechanics. Easy to read.	10	8	7	6	5	Not if final draft form. Errors in spelling and/or punctuation that make it hard to read.
4. Well organized. Clear opening that gets reader involved. Well defined middle. Clear end that leaves reader with positive impression concerning a major point.	10	8	7	6	5	Not organized well. Not a clear beginning, middle and end. End does not leave writer with an idea of a major point.
5. The personal qualities that the writer admires in individuals are clear. It is clear what kind of people the writer feels built and shaped America.	10	8	7	6	5	It is very unclear what personal qualities the writer admires. It is very unclear what kind of people the writer feels built and shaped America.

program. You can also see the varieties of assessments which are planned for students, as performances, portfolios, oral presentations, and group work are all mentioned in the philosophy statement. Developing a statement like this and distributing it to parents, students, teachers, and administrations is highly recommended. It makes clear what the purposes of your assessment program are and establishes how student work will be measured.

Examining the *Essential Question Project Spring 1994*, we can see how the Humanities team operationalizes their philosophy. First and foremost, the curriculum is driven by questions. We can imagine what the course content might have been by simply reviewing the three Essential Questions students are asked to address. What becomes evident in our review are the endless possibilities for building curriculum around questions such as these.

Who built America? Consider how many ways this question can be interpreted and how many curricular directions you might pursue. We could study the pure physical growth of the country — roads, railroads, river highways, the growth of cities, and so on. Or, what of the economic implications of the question: laborers or capitalists? Immigrant workers? This, of course, relates directly to the second question: *How have women and minorities helped to build America?* But again, let's consider the many directions we could travel in: Politically? Socially? Culturally? The curriculum, like American History itself, becomes interpretive — and students can become much more active shapers of their lessons. Consider, too, the kinds of *checkpoint* assignments and assessments which would have to be developed for such a curriculum.

Finally, consider the third question: *How will you continue to shape America?* As with so many of the other assessments we have examined, and the previous Exhibition presented in this chapter, the work ultimately comes back to the students and their own experiences. How will they *apply* what they are learning? How will the skills and knowledge of this curriculum translate into their real world? That dimension of performance assessment is the one so often ignored or neglected in traditional testing and assessment, and is a major reason students feel disconnected from their schooling.

Consider how this Exhibition invites students to participate in their education and look at the *outcomes* it aims for. Aside from the third Essential Question, which directly addresses the student, this Exhibition asks students to work with others, to write a personal reflection, to include historical and fictional figures in a work of their own creation, and to present written and oral work publicly. Beyond that, they must write a letter which specifically directs students to consider not only their world as part of a historical continuum but to also consider *who* they are — and might be — in that world!

If we examine the rubrics for the Group and Individual Projects (which were also used for peer and self-evaluations), we can focus on the outcomes and expectations for the Hibberd students. The Group rubric highlights the following outcomes: strong presentation skills; presenting evidence for historical statements; developing incisive questioning skills (and the ability to field those questions); using multimedia to present ideas; documenting sources accurately; and carefully preparing work. The Individual rubric not only reinforces those areas, but also puts a clear premium on clear, creative, mechanically proficient, and well-organized writing.

So, while the *outcomes* may not have been enunciated in the assignment, the rubrics and the performances required present the broad picture of what students would be expected to know and be able to do. We can also be assured that students have seen similar assignments and rubrics throughout the school year. There is no element of "surprise!" when students are presented with a final Exhibition such as this. As important, there is a consistent element in this Exhibition — from the reflective writing to the personal letter to the self-evaluation — which directly addresses **the student** and acknowledges the importance of that individual's making sense of the Essential Questions, the content, and the purpose of his or her schooling.

In creating and presenting their work, students are invested in what they are doing. Their labor is aimed at reflecting who they are, what they think, how they make sense of history, literature, the current world. The stakes are high and the expectations lofty, too, but, as the Hibberd statement points out:

> Assessment is an ongoing process whether done by teachers, by students assessing the work of peers, or students doing self-assessment. Assessment must be timely and frequent. It does not measure, but helps improve, gives models, pro-

vides opportunities for feedback, and allows opportunities for successive approximation.

This commitment to student improvement, with its focus on the students first, is a key element to designing successful Exhibitions and performance assessments. If our goals are not clear it will be hard to know if we have reached them or not. Hibberd's Exhibition is a fine guidepost for us to follow.

PERFORMANCES TO EXHIBITIONS: THREE SYSTEMS

To get a broader picture of how a performance assessment system operates, we are going to revisit three schools previously presented. In Chapter 2, the *performances* chapter, we saw how Fulton Valley Prep/Piner High School, Bronxville High School, and Heathwood Hall Episcopal School created performance-based assessments for their students. It was pointed out that these are *checkpoints*, assessments designed to help students prepare for the more broad-based, nonroutine, complex problems they will face not only in their academic future, but throughout their lives. So, performance assessments in Science can still be stepping-stones to achievement in the Humanities, and vice versa. The idea behind a performance assessment *system* is that students are required to show what they know and can do in a variety of ways and across disciplinary borders. The focus is on student performance and improvement, and the disciplines, if focused on *skills outcomes* together, can support one another in this effort.

We will examine a Humanities Exhibition from Fulton Valley Prep, taking note how the *skills* work required of students dovetails nicely with the Science project presented in Chapter 2. In the case of Bronxville High School, we will look at the Final Exhibition required of 9th graders, noting how the earlier performances were appropriate *checkpoints* in preparing students for this Exhibition. Finally, we will examine Heathwood Hall's first attempt at Graduation by Exhibition, looking at their *Senior Exhibitions Handbook,* and noting how the earlier example of the Humanities performances (Chapter 2) would help prepare students for this final Exhibition.

HEROES AT FULTON VALLEY PREP

Piner High School's Humanities team at Fulton Valley Prep designed their curriculum (Fig. 3.3) around quarterly Exhibitions. In doing so, the team subscribed to several consistent practices, well worth noting.

◆ As you will see, the Exhibition is presented in the same format — as the Science performance used: "Where are we going?" "How will we get there?" "How will we know if we've arrived?" Once again, this simple approach, presented *before any work commences* makes the curriculum clear to students.

◆ The Exhibition is driven by an *Essential Question*. In clarifying curriculum to students, an important shift which performance assessments make is to focus work around a question or theme, as opposed to giving the students the impression that curriculum *is* content. The concept that content is material to be wrestled with, questioned, and applied to problems, is an important distinction performance assessments make — and certainly a shift from traditional models of the past.

◆ Students are given *choices* as to what they will present and how they will present it. This *does not* mean that students are not responsible for the spectrum of work which is "covered" during the period they are preparing for their Exhibition. It simply means they will be allowed to exercise critical judgment about how they best believe they can respond to the Essential Question and present their progress in acquiring habits of mind.

◆ Students are expected to be *reflective* learners. As with the earlier Science performance, a requirement of both this Exhibition is "Letter Journals." Basically, students keep running records/logs of their own thinking about the progress of their work toward answering the Essential Question and making sense of the content being studied.

(Text continues on page 92.)

FIGURE 3.3: FULTON VALLEY PREP — HUMANITIES CURRICULUM

Fulton Valley Prep at Piner High School
Humanities Curriculum
First quarter, Fall 1993

Where are we going?

Our first area of focus this year in Humanities will be on <u>Heroes</u>. When DC Comics allowed Superman to die in the spring of 1993 (killed by the monster "Doomsday"), social historians mourned him as "The Last American Hero." In an age of instant communication and no-holds-barred journalism, no real, live person can be a hero, they argue, because we will always learn about their flaws and errors.   But perhaps there <u>are</u> people worth admiring and imitating. Heroes may be able to help us know how to live our own lives. Our study will lead us to think about how heroes are shaped by a culture and how heroes shape the culture in which they live?   As we examine ideas about heroes and about the values of our society and ourselves, we will continually apply what we learn to our central question: "Who should our heroes be?"

How will we get there?

As we explore the central question, we will participate in an ongoing process of defining and redefining The Hero. We will seek out potential Hero/ine candidates, creating and expanding an extensive class list. We will conduct interviews and invite people from outside our class to come in and talk about their heroes. We will read a wide variety of articles, poems and short fiction and non-fiction stories, we will read Sophocles' classic *Oedipus the King,* and we will see movies which expand our notions about Heroes. Through group seminars we will deepen our understanding of ideas and improve our abilities to express and defend our points of view. We will correspond with one another in Letter Journals and will focus on the use of writing in the process of thinking.

How will we know if we've arrived?

At the conclusion of the Heroes study, each student will complete an exhibition of knowledge and skills gained during the unit. The exhibition will present and justify a collection of heroes for our time, in a format selected by the student from a menu of choices. Each student must demonstrate mastery (which will be recorded as a grade of 'B'). Some students may demonstrate a distinguished level of accomplishment (which will be recorded as a grade of 'A.')

HEROES Exhibition
A Collection of Heroes
Rubric

	Mastery (B)	Distinguished (A)
PROJECT CONTENT	1. The project contains a clear, thoughtful definition of a hero for our society.	1. The project contains a clear, thoughtful, multi-faceted definition of a hero for our society.
	2. The project includes a collection of heroes who fit the author's definition.	2. The project includes a varied collection of heroes who fit the author's definition.
	3. Each hero in the collection is described accurately and connections between the heroes and the definition are evident.	3. Each hero in the collection is described accurately and in detail and connections between the heroes and the definition are clearly drawn.
	4. The author has researched the heroes in the collection and has included a bibliography of sources.	4. The author has thoroughly researched the heroes in the collection and has included a bibliography of sources.

Note: The size of the collection (number of heroes) should be related both to the choice of format and the depth of descriptions. E.g. a calendar would show 12 heroes and trading cards probably 12-15, while a speech or monologue series would present 3-4 heroes in greater depth.

PROJECT FORMAT	1. Written material is the original creation of the author or is clearly labeled as a quotation with the source identified. 2. Written materials are organized and readable, with an introduction, body and conclusion. Hypercard stacks allow easy travel among cards. 3. Written materials are neatly hand-written in ink or typed and contain few spelling, punctuation or usage errors. 4. The layout and graphics in an anthology, calendar, cards, magazine or mural are neat and easy to follow. 5. The performer (series of monologues or speech) speaks clearly and loudly and, although using a script, shows evidence of ample rehearsal.	1. Written material is the original creation of the author or is clearly labeled as a quotation with the source identified. 2. Written materials are well-organized and interesting, with an introduction, body and conclusion. Hypercard stacks allow easy travel among cards and use graphics and backgrounds creatively. 3. Written materials are typed and contain minimal spelling, punctuation or usage errors. 4. The layout and graphics in an anthology, calendar, cards, magazine or mural are creative, eye-catching and professional-looking. 5. The performer (series of monologues or speech) speaks clearly and loudly and has memorized the material, referring minimally to note cards. The presentation is energetic, believable and convincing.
DEFENSE	1. The presenter can explain reasons for his/her definition and can field questions about the heroes in the collection.	1. The presenter can explain connections between his/her definition and our society and can thoroughly defend her/his choice of heroes for the collection.

HEROES Exhibition

What kind of heroes would you prescribe for our society?
After whom should we pattern our lives?

For this exhibition, you will create and justify a collection of heroes for our time and culture.
In your project you will define your idea of a hero for late 20th century America, based on your own interpretation and synthesis of class activities. You will select a group of persons–mythic or real, living or dead, famous or known only to a few– who exemplify that definition. You will have the opportunity to choose the format of your project from a list which follows. Finally, you will make an oral presentation of your collection, first to a small group of your peers and then to the whole class, during which you will explain and defend your ideas more completely, focusing on our central question: *Who Should Our Heroes Be?*

1. **Think** about the articles, poems, stories, and books you read, the movies you see, and the seminars you join. Think some more. Think on your way to and from school. Think as you are going to sleep. Think in the shower. Throughout the various class activities, keep your focus on two main ideas: (1) What is a hero and (2) Who is a hero?

2. **Write down your ideas frequently.**
   • Keep your own list of definitions of "the hero."
   • Write notes to yourself as you try to define and redefine a hero for today.
   • Keep your own list of potential heroes, including descriptions, in addition to the class lists.
   • Write often about your ideas in letters to other students and to the teacher.

3. **Decide on a format** for your project. You may choose from the following list:

   a. anthology of stories and poems, original and found   *[includes author's introduction]*

   b. series of monologues   *[includes performer's introduction]*

   c. expository speech   *[includes intro, body, conclusion]*

   d. illustrated calendar   *[plus promotional copy]*

   e. set of trading cards   *[plus promotional copy]*

   f. illustrated magazine or comic book   *[includes author's introduction]*

   g. hypercard stack   *[includes author's introduction]*

   h. mural   *[with legend and artist's notes]*

4. **Write an exhibition proposal**, which includes:

   a. your working **definition** of "the hero"

   b. a working list of **heroes** you plan to include

     NOTE: Both 'a' and 'b' may change as you develop your exhibition.

   c. the **format** of your project

   d. a list of **materials** needed

   e. a **bibliography** of sources you have consulted and plan to consult

   f. a **timeline**, including estimated dates of presentation to your work group and to the class.

5. **Make an appointment** with your teacher and your work group to **review** your exhibition proposal.

6. After your proposal is approved, **proceed** with your plan.

7. When your project is finished, schedule a **preliminary presentation** meeting with your teacher and your work group to receive constructive criticism before your final exhibition.

8. Schedule your **exhibition**, which includes a public presentation and defense of your project.

EXHIBITION DEADLINE: _____

♦ Finally, there is a rubric presented to students *at the
   beginning* of the project — long before any work is due.
   It cannot be emphasized enough how important this
   is. And, while rubrics are difficult to devise — and early
   versions often seem painfully lacking, as we learn to
   design them better with experience — the time spent
   is well worth the effort in helping students to focus on
   goals and expectations. It is also a fairness issue —
   students have a right to know what their work will be
   judged against. Too often — and standardized tests are
   guilty of this again and again — students haven't the
   foggiest notion of what the standard of excellence or
   outstanding achievement is. Again, rubrics are difficult
   to create and are often criticized as being too "subjective," but that is an argument for investigation in a later
   chapter. The point here is that almost any rubric can
   clearly serve the student's interest better than no rubric
   at all!

In examining the Fulton Valley Prep Exhibitions, consider not
only what students are required to do to be successful in their writing
and presentations, but also consider what they *must have had to have
done* to be prepared to tackle the assignment. Also note what role(s)
the teacher plays in coaching students toward their goals. And,
of course, take note of how *the student is the responsible party* throughout the Exhibition. It is up to the student to make choices, to schedule
appointments, to find materials, to get constructive feedback, and
so on. In all, this is a challenging Exhibition, geared toward students
demonstrating what they have learned across the skills, content,
and attitudinal domains. By looking carefully at the assignments,
we can come to some clear conclusions about the outcomes, expectations, standards, and amount of work students at Fulton Valley
Prep engage in.

WHAT DO THEY KNOW? WHAT CAN THEY DO?

Let's review the Fulton Valley Prep Exhibitions from a purely
categorical approach. That is, let's consider what skills, what content,
and what attitudes or dispositions students would have to *exhibit*
to successfully complete this assignment. In doing so, we will have

to carefully review the rubric, too, noting what "Distinguished" performance is described as.

+ *Skills*

Reading, writing, speaking, and listening are always the skills which *outcome statements* rattle off, of course. But looking at FVP's Exhibition we can see that these assignments do, in fact, require students to demonstrate those skills. As important, a series of problemsolving and critical thinking skills are also demanded of students: How do we define a hero? Who is a hero? What would be the best format for presenting one's ideas?

In tackling those questions, students will have to exercise more than simple reading, writing, speaking, listening skills. The ability to work effectively and efficiently with other people is another outcome in the skills domain which students would have to engage in. And, if we needed further clarification regarding *skills* expectations, we could always refer to the rubrics.

+ *Content*

The *Heroes* Exhibition has variety of readings in the content area, including *Oedipus the King, A Man for All Seasons, Death of a Salesman, The Natural,* and *One Flew Over the Cuckoo's Nest.* As noted in the assignment, there are also nonfiction articles, poems, and movies included in this curriculum. Some choices about content are made by teachers; sometimes students can exert their own control over areas of content and curriculum. The point is that much of this **leads to** more content, but that it is often driven *by the students.* In designing their Exhibition, students will have to raise content questions, do research, evaluate and analyze materials, synthesize concepts, and so on. The fact that they need to *construct* their knowledge and understanding of content is what gives Exhibitions like these power. Knowing the expectation for "Mastery" and "Distinguished" work gives the students a clear target to shoot for.

+ *Attitude/Disposition*

Throughout both this Exhibition, students would be expected to demonstrate the following qualities:

- *Responsibility* — The burden of work is on the student's shoulders; she or he must produce.

- *Time Management* — There are clear deadlines noted. While this may be considered a "skill," very often a students approach to time management is attitudinal, and an Exhibition like this tends to merge that "skill" with the sense of responsibility expected of students.

- *Respect* — There are many instances where students are working with others, listening to others, and so on which require respectful attitudes and behavior.

- *Independence* — Students will have to demonstrate an ability to work by themselves, to produce work independently, to accept the responsibility for independent thinking.

- *Reflection* — Students are asked to keep Learning Journals, which require that they develop the *habit* of reflection. It is easy to imagine that FVP students will, by the time they graduate, rather automatically *reflect* on where they are, what they are doing, how things work, and so on.

Many more skills, much more detailed content, and an array of attitudinal/dispositional behaviors could be discussed in relation to this Exhibition. And that is part of the point about using this examples, and about presenting students with Exhibitions as part of their curriculum. These are rich and generative assignments which challenge students to show what they know and can do. They ask for reflective thinking, they ask students to be active, constructivist learners, they ask for high standards of achievement.

Cast in the light of more traditional testing and assessment, consider how this Exhibition might give a better gauge of what a student actually does know and is able to do. Consider how a student could more easily self-assess his or her work as "distinguished" or not. Consider the amount and type of work they would have to do *throughout an academic quarter* to be prepared to present this Exhibition publicly.

Students could still study some very "traditional" material, be tested on that material in a very "traditional" fashion, and still be moving toward performing an Exhibition like this. If the "traditional" material and the "traditional" testing is framed in a larger picture of what students should know and be able to do, and if that larger picture needs feedback which only a "traditional" test might provide, fine. One of the key aspects of designing Exhibitions is to start with those *outcomes* you believe students will need to demonstrate *and then* plan how you will incorporate the skills, content, and attitude materials and work for the students.

Commitment to this assessment system asks teachers to be reflective, to consider what is important for students *to demonstrate* clearly and publicly that they know and can do. Teachers then design assessment, curriculum, and instruction to serve that end. Fulton Valley Prep provides a fine model for exactly that.

APPLYING WHAT THEY LEARN: A 9TH GRADE EXHIBITION

In Chapter 2, on *performances*, we saw how Bronxville High School 9th graders learned basic geography and developed content knowledge by way of two "travel agent" simulation assessments. By the time June rolled around, these students were expected to not only have a sense of the progress of Western Civilization, but to also have steadily improved their skills as readers, writers, public speakers, listeners, group participants, and so on. Because the course had an interdisciplinary focus, students were also expected to make and see connections between Language Arts, Social Studies, and Art throughout the development of Western culture. The challenge, then, was to create a Final Exhibition which would address the 9th grade outcomes *and* have relevance and meaning to the students. Since the Bosnian crisis was raging in the Spring of 1993, the teaching team decided that some *connection* between the study of Western Civilization and that crisis should serve as the organizing theme for the Final Exhibition.

The need to *apply* the skills, content, and attitudes/behaviors which had been worked on throughout the year was a paramount objective for the teaching team (Linda Passman, Mary Schenck, and myself). So, with an eye toward the original list of "9th Grade Exit Outcomes," a review of the content which had been studied, and a concern for attaining relevance, the team set about designing a Final Exhibition.

In reviewing this Exhibition, take note of the attempt by the designers to keep the design simple but the challenge complex. Considering the developmental level of 9th grade students, as well as the range of student abilities (it was a heterogeneous group), the Final Exhibition had to be clear and direct, yet require students to apply an array of skills and content knowledge. The decision was made to create two distinct parts to the Final Exhibition — a written component based on the course's materials and on current materials about Bosnia, and an oral component in the form of a series of Socratic Seminars which would require *application* of the written segment. What we will examine below (Fig. 3.4) will only discuss the written component of the Final Exhibition.

In examining the written part of this Exhibition, what becomes evident is that students were assessed not only on their final product — the letters/position papers to President Clinton — but also on their *process*. Looking at the schedule which is included as part of the assessment, one will notice that students had a full week to develop their Rough Draft and that during their in-class time (which were 94-minute blocks of time), there were two, and sometimes three, teachers present to coach. Again, the importance of students *doing the work* and teachers serving as advisors, critics, coaches throughout the process, cannot be emphasized enough. If we expect students to achieve high standards and reach the outcomes which are set for them, **they** must be the active agents during the educational process. Teacher "performance" *must* be that of the coach, the resource (and provider of resources), the friendly critic, the advisor — not dispenser of content knowledge.

In this case, students had been through enough *checkpoints*, like the earlier "travel agent" performances, that they knew how to get to work at the process.

In reviewing this Final Exhibition, then, one is asked to:

♦ Review the 9th Grade Exit Outcomes to see if they can be identified in the assignment. Are they embedded in the tasks?

♦ Take note of what students would have to do to succeed at this Exhibition. Examine the Criteria for writing.

♦ Note the choices students had and evaluate whether this would, in fact, enable teachers to clearly gauge what students knew and could do.

(Text continues on page 101.)

FIGURE 3.4: BRONXVILLE HIGH SCHOOL — EXHIBITION

Exit Outcomes
9th Grade
Bil Johnson

Skills & Habits
- Research
- Writing in a variety of modes
- Analytical reading
- Working cooperatively in a group setting
- Working independently
- Effective listening
- Ability to speak publicly
- Effective time management
- Organization of materials, readings, etc.
- Good study habits
- Effective questioning
- Group discussion

Content
- The G.R.E.A.S.E.S. analytical model (Government, Religion, Economics, Art/Architecture, Science/Technology, Education, Social/Cultural Values) to understand cultures over time and geographic locations
- The foundations of Western Civilization, using the analytical model. Understanding where "we" (United States) come from.
- Basic cause-and-effect --- the flow of history as logical & predictable (if you know how to look)
- Art/architecutre appreciation
- Knowing primary/secondary sources
- Current events

Attitudes / Behaviors
- Responsible
- Open-minded
- Fair-minded
- Courteous, respectful
- Curiosity
- Reflective

Essential Questions
- How did we (the U.S.) get here?
- What is a good society/civilization?
- What is a fair or just society?
- What is a good citizen?

Final Exhibition Preparation
A/B Interdisc

The Problem you will be faced with:
You will be asked to respond to a simple task ---- cooling down one of the world's hottest spots! The Bosnian Conflict is clearly out of control and no one seems to know what to do. So, you are going to help. Based on your knowledge of literature, history, and art, you are going to prepare position papers which will advise the U.S. government on what course of action it needs to take to help resolve the Bosnian Crisis.

The Process you will follow:
You will need to read/review various sources you have read/studied this year, or have been given in the last few weeks. Based on those sources/readings, etc. you will devise a position which you believe the U.S. should take on the Bosnian crisis ---- *from the point of view of the* SOURCE (whether it's an author, a figure from history, an artist, whomever)! You will cite *specific textual evidence* to support your position. In all, you will write three in-class position statements (one English source, one Social Studies source, one Art source) over three days (probably June 9,10,11).

READINGS FOR BOSNIAN CRISIS

You will receive a packet of readings about the Bosnian Crisis. You must read **ALL** of the packet in order to be prepared to write an intelligent essay from any point of view, and to participate in the Class Discussion/Seminar (Part Two of the Final Exhibition on June 14 & 15).

Part Two of the Exhibition
You will be expected to articulately express advice to the U.S. government as to what its course of action in the Bosnian Crisis should be from **TWO (or more)** points of view: a) the point of view of historical (and/or literary &/or artistic) figures;
       b) your own point of view.

All points of view must be supported by **FACTUAL EVIDENCE & LOGICAL INFERENCE!**

Final Exhibition
TASKS
A/B Interdisc

1. Read material on Bosnia (class work). Become familiar with issues
    such as:
  - countries involved
  - Geography of the region
  - religions & their histories
  - reasons for disputes/conflicts
        How did it start? Chronology?
        What has happened in last year or two?
  - Other countries involved or affected.
  - Proposed solutions --- from:
        ° UN °US   °European Nations   ° Serbs
        ° Bosnians   ° The Vance-Owen Treaty proposal

2. Develop a position for each literary & historical character & artist
    as to which of the proposed solutions they would most likely
    agree with ---- what would they recommend to President
    Clinton and why?

	UN	US	Vance-Owen	Serbs	Bosnians
Literary					
Historic					
Artist					

3. Write a paper based on the following format:
    I. Intro/explanation of Bosnian Conflict
    II. Literary figure's advice **w/evidence, support**
    III. Historic figure's advice **w/evidence, support**
    {IV. Artist's advice **w/evidence, support}**
    V. Conclusions {possible scenarios if Clinton takes above advice}
      Which solution might be most effective & why? Who should
      he listen to & why?

Writing Assessment Criteria

Exemplary/Excellent ("A")

- Good use of accurate details (intelligently selective)
- Interesting - appeals to a wide audience
- Clearly makes its points, doesn't run-on or ramble
- Appropriate vocabularly / Good diction
- Correct mechanics, clear knowledge of mechanics
- Well-organized
- Smooth transitions

Good ("B")

- Appropriate use of details (some lacking)
- Attempts to appeal to a wide audience; style is basically "smooth"
- Clear thesis, makes its points with an occasional run-on
- Vocabulary is adequate; little or no mis-use of words
- Occasional mechanical errors
- Generally well-organized; some problem with transitions

Acceptable ("C")

- Misuse or lack of detail in significant places
- Transitions are weak or missing in places
- Narrow point of view; appeals to a limited audience
- Point *may* be distinct/clear BUT needs more support or details
- Organized but lacks focus, details (Doesn't clearly follow thesis at times)
- Limited vocabulary
- Mechanical errors.

Unacceptable ("D"/"F")

- Failure to use details or facts effectively
- Rambles, runs-on
- Poorly organized
- Simplistic vocabulary, misused or inappropriate diction
- Numerous mechanical errors
- No clear thesis or point of view

- ◆ Does the Exhibition ask for students to exercise Habits of Mind (evidence, connections, relevance, conjecture, perspective) and to consider the Essential Questions for the course?

- ◆ How might this Exhibition be improved upon, if it were to be done again, so that teachers and students could gather even better evidence of student progress and achievement? (In other words, does the Exhibition adequately address skills, content, and attitude outcomes or could modifications in the design make it more effective?)

The need to critique performance assessments *after* they have been given is a crucial aspect to their design. The point is **not** to "come up with" a fine set of questions which can be given year after year to test student "mastery" of content knowledge. Because the desired outcomes are complex and span a wide variety of skills, content, and behaviors, the Final Exhibition, by necessity, must be multitasked and complex. It must be reexamined constantly and modified after each use. Next year's students will *not* be like this year's, other than being in the same grade and having the same course name appearing on their schedule. The curriculum design, the instructional strategies, the assessment tools, *must* be flexible enough to not only adapt to the differences our students bring with them, but to constantly improve student performance!

How did We do? The Teachers' Perspective

Providing a glimpse at how teachers review their assessments, not only by looking at the quality of the student work produced, but by carefully scrutinizing the Exhibition design in light of the desired outcomes, is instructive. It reminds us that the purpose of performance assessments is *not only* to improve student performance, but also to provide teachers with feedback about the efficacy of their curriculum and assessment designs.

In this case, we found that the broadly stated outcomes were certainly embedded in the design of the Exhibition. The two parts of the Final Exhibition addressed all 12 of the "Skills & Habits" Exit Outcomes which had been articulated at the beginning of the year. The degree to which the students had "mastered" those outcomes, of course, became the tale of the tape, as it were. Simply designing an assessment which requires students to apply the desired skills and habits outcomes is not enough — how *well* have the students done the work? That is where teachers can begin measuring the effectiveness of their program. And it is where students can also measure their own progress.

In the same way, the Content and Attitudes/Behaviors Exit Outcomes could be reviewed and evaluated. Because the Outcomes are broadly stated, and do not include more detail regarding Language Arts and Art Outcomes (students had received those separately, earlier in the year), we can only offer the cursory comment that those outcomes which are listed in the Social Studies segment were addressed in the task design — and if not explicitly, students inferred which analytical models were appropriate and so on.

The question which arises again, of course, is "how well" did students do in achieving those outcomes and how does student achievement inform teachers about their curriculum, instruction, and assessment design? In this case, while there was a range of achievement, students performed at what the team considered "proficient" levels to extremely "distinguished" levels, depending upon the task, the student's interest in and ability for it, and the amount of teacher-coaching which could be made available. But there were some noticeable problems which the teaching team needed to address.

The Writing Assessment Criteria was problematic. While the next chapter will go into depth regarding the kinds of problems rubrics pose, it is worth examining this example to set the stage for that discussion. While the Criteria presents students with some useful guidelines regarding expectations, there is not enough *definition of terms* to make it as helpful as they could be. And, while students were asked to respond to these Criteria as part of a self-evaluation — and had been using similar rubrics throughout the year — there is still a problem with clarity: What are "accurate details" as opposed to "appropriate use of details," for example? Some answers to these questions were garnered during coaching periods with students, certainly, but overall, this was an area vastly in need of redesign, revision, and rewriting. While student input is valuable and important in this area, it is still incumbent upon teachers to devise rubrics and criteria — with appropriate benchmark examples to refer to — which make expectations as clear as possible to students.

The choices offered students in this Exhibition proved quite revealing and served the team's objectives. Because students could decide *who* would write letters to President Clinton, the teaching team was provided with interesting insights to student perspectives on literary characters, historical figures, and notable artists. That students worked hard to achieve distinct "voices" while fashioning their arguments, made the assignment all the more interesting for both the teachers and the students. And, while offering students choices *could* lead to narrowly focused responses — using a writer, historical personage, and artist from the same time period, for example — that scenario never emerged; students used the sweep of history to choose quite liberally. More often than not, they seemed to use a broad overview to find those writers, historical characters, and artists who could best express the student's *own* point of view to the President.

Finally, this Exhibition clearly addressed the habits of mind the team was striving for while implicitly asking students to respond to the essential questions about fair and just societies, "good" societies/civilizations, and how the U.S. got to where it is today. Throughout the Exhibition students were required to examine perspectives and viewpoints, evaluate and present evidence, make connections from literature to history to art and across historical time periods, as well as note the relevance of the task at hand. The entire Socratic Seminar experience was one of conjecture.

Was this a successful Final Exhibition? Certainly. Was it without flaws? Certainly not. Yet, compared to simply taking a 3-hour block of time some June morning, sitting students in a gymnasium with countless rows of desks, and asking them to answer some multiple-choice questions and write an "essay," this is a much better assessment to gauge student progress toward the 9th Grade Exit Outcomes. Yes, it requires more time, more thought, more *work*, in general, to initially design a Final Exhibition like this, *but* it is far more valuable for both the teachers and the students. Final Exhibitions like the ones presented here are not designed for calculating a "quick grade" to send students packing for vacation. They are part of a thoughtful process which integrates curriculum and instruction design with assessments, aiming at making students more active participants in the process of their own education.

Recent surveys indicate that the American public is wary of "innovations," and concerned students will not be schooled in the "basics." Yet, these same surveys reflect a public which wants higher standards and a more challenging curriculum. Performance assessments are not a panacea, but they are a clear path toward higher standards, more challenging curriculum, and insuring that students do, in fact, leave school well-versed in the "basics."

Those who make a commitment to developing and implementing performance assessments like the Final Exhibitions presented here, *must* be wise politically. The public *must be included* in these decisions; they *must be educated* as to why and how these assessments will create higher standards, will challenge and engage students, and will insure that students master fundamentals on the way to developing complex skills. Just as an important element of every Exhibition is the *public presentation* by students, those teachers and administrators who believe in attaining that kind of public accountability through student performance must recognize that *public inclusion* and *public dialogue* are necessary first steps in the process. It is a small but crucial initial gambit; one which can result in greater energy, enthusiasm, and excitement from students, teachers, *and* the community when the Final Exhibitions are presented. The point here is simple: In the excitement of creating performance assessments or exhibition projects, significant steps can be forgotten or overlooked — not just in the assessment design, but in the *process* of creating the performance assessment system. Going into that process with eyes open, ears attuned, and clear information to disseminate, can ultimately help everyone achieve a very common goal — better performance, more enthusiastic participation, and higher achievement from our students.

TAKING THE RISK: HEATHWOOD HALL'S SENIOR EXHIBITION

At some point, it is time to put up or shut up. When considering innovations and risk-taking, the moment comes when we have to jump in the deep end and see what happens. For Heathwood Hall Episcopal School, the early 1990s had been a period of innovation and change. The staff had committed itself to performance assessments and begun the conversation about Graduation-by-Exhibition. Things were going well, students were achieving, the community was supportive. A decision was made — talk about

Senior Exhibitions could *always* continue, but1993–94 became the time to act. The Class of 1994 at Heathwood Hall would publicly present Senior Exhibitions in the Spring.

Because the Senior Exhibition had been a topic of sustained conversation for a number of years, the staff at Heathwood Hall had some clear ideas about what they believed would be a representative Final Exhibition for their students. Nonetheless, time and effort was needed to commit those ideas to paper — the students and the community needed to see a clear statement about the *why* and the *how* of a Senior Exhibition.

The *Senior Exhibitions Handbook* provides a clear statement as to purpose and philosophy; the expected outcomes are clear. Not only that, but the guidelines for students are delineated in a manner that defines the Exhibition, yet leaves room for student choice. As with all the Exhibitions studied here, the responsibility is the student's. The support of the staff is evident throughout but the student, if she or he is to graduate, must take the initiative.

In reviewing Heathwood Hall's *Senior Exhibitions Handbook* (Fig. 3.5) there are several salient points to note.

♦ The philosophical statement which frames all that follows and presents the school's graduation expectations for its students.

♦ The clearly defined First Semester task (the Autobiographic Portfolio) and the clearly defined Second Semester task (the Senior Thesis).

♦ The Essential Questions used to focus student work.

♦ The articulated rubric and the Standards statement.

♦ A well-defined timeline of "Critical Dates."

Because the Senior Exhibition is carefully monitored by faculty members, students are guided each step of the way. So, while graduating students by exhibition can seem a daunting task, Heathwood Hall, in its first attempt, has created a template which is worth considering. They have taken their philosophical principles, considered their desired outcomes, decided what assessment instruments would allow students to demonstrate their levels of progress, and created a clear guideline for their students and the community.

(Text continues on page 113.)

FIGURE 3.5: HEATHWOOD HALL — SENIOR EXHIBITION HANDBOOK

I. Introduction and Philosophy

Heathwood Hall was founded in 1951, and its mission has evolved to what it is today:

Children are a precious gift from God to the world. We believe, therefore, that our mission is caring for the education and development of the group of young people enrolled at Heathwood Hall Episcopal School. Our purpose is to guide them toward becoming successful, fulfilled and healthy adults who realize the need to generate the same kind of beneficence in the lives and in the communities of others.

As a part of the School's mission, we affirm the nine principles of the **Coalition of Essential Schools**, of which we have been a member school since 1987. Those ideas are listed here:

1. We want our students to use their minds well.
2. We want to have a few relatively simple goals, vigorously pursued.
3. The goals are universal, though the means to these goals will vary with every class and every grade.
4. Learning is personalized to the individual student.
5. The guiding metaphor of our school is Student as Worker, which necessitates the role of teacher as coach.
6. Graduation from the school is by Exhibition of Mastery, not just by completion of a number of units.
7. The school is characterized by a tone of decency.
8. Teachers at Heathwood Hall are expected to be generalists, not specialists.
9. The school will operate within a balanced budget.

Habits of Heart and Mind

It follows that the fundamental aim of Heathwood's upper school is to teach students to use their minds well, and to prepare them to live productive, socially useful and personally satisfying lives. The school's academic program stresses intellectual development, and we affirm the importance of emotional, physical and spiritual health in our students, their families, our faculty and our staff. To this end, six "habits of heart and mind" are stressed.

(1) Each student becomes an independent, inquisitive thinker, and ultimately a life-long learner by taking ownership for his/her education.
(2) Each student is able to see patterns and make connections.
(3) Each students accepts that there are many cultural perspectives from which to view art, literature, foreign languages, science, mathematics, politics, economics, or faith.
(4) Each student values sustained quiet time for reflection, reading and study.

(5) Each student sees tasks through to their completion and reacts positively to setbacks.

(6) All members of this learning community work cooperatively in the pursuit of common intellectual goals.

Graduation Requirements

All graduation requirements will remain the same for the classes of 1994 and 1995, though each student in these classes must successfully complete the exhibitions of mastery, as approved by the Board of Trustees. The first semester portfolio will be the focal point of English 12. All of the research components will be started under the aegis of each student's advisor.

Successful completion of each portion of the exhibitions will result in one full credit, a half credit for each.

II. Semester One: The Autobiographic Portfolio

So that our seniors understand their skills, strengths and talents better, and in order to enhance the college admissions process, they will create and compile an autobiographic portfolio, to include written and visual components.

Essential questions, like the ones below, will inspire students to begin thinking about the scope and nature of their portfolios. Students may write their own questions which address issues of identity, place, society, family, etc. These questions should be used as a "starting place" for their autobiographic writings.

1. How does the geographical region(s) in which you are raised help define who you are?
2. How do I want to be remembered?
3. How do I fit into a pluralistic society?
4. How has my relationship to my neighborhood, church, family, school, or peers shaped who I am?

Assessment of the portfolio and the Senior Thesis will be by a committee consisting of the following people: one outside adult, one faculty advisor (assigned), one junior from your advisor group, a second faculty member, and an outside "expert." (EC = the student's Exhibition Committee)

The portfolio will include:

1. **College Essay(s)** -- Each student will be expected to include at least one college admissions essay in his/her portfolio. This essay(s) may be autobiographical or build on any other piece or interest explored in the portfolio. Each student

should strive to select his/her best piece of writing. If you have several essays, of which you are proud, then each should be included.

2. **A Post-Graduate Plan** which accounts for the whole person. (Body, Mind, Spirit) -- This piece of the portfolio is intended to be a logical extension of the college counselor's "brag sheet." Each student must develop a plan that describes his/her current purpose for earning a diploma. Reflecting on purposes helps to set goals. This plan can give direction to all subsequent work during first and second semester. It may be updated any time during first semester, though a first draft will be attempted early in first semester. Your advisor should be apprised of any and all changes.

3. **A Written Autobiography** -- This piece should be reflective of self and will be the central product of English 12. These autobiographies may draw on genealogies, family histories or any other pertinent information about your life. They may assume the form of any literary genre, though conventions and standards of that genre will be applied.

4. **A Non-Written Component** – This piece should also be reflective of self, but it will be realized through a medium other than writing. This piece may build on any aspect of the written autobiography, or may "speak to" a previously unaddressed aspect of your life. All artistic and technological media are welcome.

5. **The Proposal for Senior Thesis** -- The written proposal for the second semester exhibition, to be submitted during the first semester to the EC and advisor, will include:
•a detailed statement regarding the scope and purpose of the project
•an annotated bibliography
•a one page abstract on the research process (i.e. How do you plan to investigate this topic?)
•a rationale for the value of the project (Who cares?).

6. **Written Reflection** on the question, "How does what I do reflect who I am?" This should be the last item completed during first semester.

Rubric for Assessment of Autobiographic Portfolio

No public presentation is required.

Work is submitted to the advisor and the English 12 teacher on or before the due date, as specified on the checklist. The portfolio will be circulated to and reviewed by each member of the EC.

The student will then meet with her EC and offer answers/comments to questions or observations made by the members of the EC. A student may choose to present a piece of his/her work, or simply respond to comments. When the EC is satisfied, the meeting will conclude with a determination of a grade for the work. Grading for the portfolio will be arrived at by consensus. The descriptors are as follows:

Distinctive — Portfolios that meet all criteria described below and surpass those criteria in inventiveness, creativity and risk-taking will be designated distinctive.

Competent — Contains all required material. Meets due dates. Shows reflection and thoughtfulness. Could be viewed by a "stranger" and that person would know you better. The non-written component complements the written materials. All written work should reflect the following qualities: cohesiveness, creativity, originality, command of grammar and mechanics, consistency with selected genre , voice, style, diction.

Unacceptable — Incomplete, disorganized, and poorly planned portfolios which show a chronic disregard for due dates. **Students must resubmit unacceptable portfolios by Friday, January 14, 1994. One re-submission is allowed. A student will not graduate in June if a competent portfolio is not submitted by January 14th.**

III. Semester Two: Senior Thesis

The second semester exhibition will draw on the student's interests, beliefs, and/or post-graduate plans. It must have an intellectual focus, must be authentic, must demonstrate sustained and substantive research, must demonstrate a solid knowledge of the academic area(s) chosen for the exhibition, and must include use of resources beyond the Heathwood community. Two products will result from this work.

1. **A Free-Standing Research Paper** — A student will write a research paper, appropriate in length to the topic being investigated, and may create an original work. This work must draw upon his/her research and any original work submitted must include a written defense or explanation based upon that research.

2. **An Oral Presentation** — A student will present his/her findings orally, during the Senior Thesis Symposium, to be held in late April. The purpose of this presentation will be for the student to share the gist of his/her findings in 20-30 minute sessions, and to field any questions. The presentation should summarize the work, its significance, what was learned at its conclusion and along the way. These sessions will be open to the entire Heathwood and Columbia communities, and attendance will be required for underclassmen.

Rubric and Evaluation Standards for the Senior Thesis

Assessment of the written and oral components will be conducted by the student's EC following the Senior Thesis Symposium. As with the autobiographic portfolio, the members of the EC will evaluate the student's by consensus and use the descriptors which follow. The Senior Thesis will be assessed wholistically, in that one evaluation will be given for the two components.

Distinctive - *Without exception*, written and oral components will be submitted on time. The thesis will have a clear intellectual focus, will use resources beyond the Heathwood community, will show a basic knowledge of the academic area(s) selected, and will combine the student's interest with substantive research. Additionally, distinctive work will surpass this criteria in inventiveness, creativity, and risk-taking. Special care will be taken in addressing the question: Who cares?

A distinctive oral presentation will be cohesive, persuasive, engaging, articulate and audible.

Competent -- Written and oral components will be submitted on time, with no chronic disregard for due dates. It will meet all writing criteria, which has been previously established (see Autobiographic Portfolio). The thesis will have a clear intellectual focus, will use resources beyond the Heathwood community, will show a basic knowledge of the academic area(s) selected, and will combine the student's interest with substantive research.

A competent oral presentation will be cohesive, persuasive, engaging, articulate and audible.

Unacceptable -- Incomplete written or oral components, and/or chronic disregard for due dates will result in the designation of unacceptable. A reminder is neccessary here. If the rough draft is deemed unacceptable, then a second draft is due March 28.

Senior Thesis Symposium

The Senior Thesis Symposium will be a three-day event including presentations by all seniors. Three will occur simultaneously: one in the auditorium and two others in Campus Center classrooms. Students may choose the location which best suits their topic and their respective strengths.

All underclassmen are required to attend presentations on Thursday, Friday and Saturday. They will have signed up to attend those exhibitions of interest to them. All members of Heathwood Hall community, as well as the general public, are invited.

Hours: Thursday, April 28: 9-11, 12-2
        Friday, April 29:   9-11, 12-2
        Saturday, April 30:   10-12

IV. Critical Dates for the Class of 1994

<u>1993</u>

Summer of 1993 -- Exhibitions Summer Institute at Heathwood Summer School

August 25, 1993 (Wednesday) -- School Opens

September 1993 -- Begin work on Portfolio in English 12

September 1993 -- Parent Meeting on Senior Exhibitions (T-shirts, food, informal atmosphere, break into advisor groups)

October 1, 1993 (Friday) -- Preliminary Senior Thesis Topic Proposal (2 paragraph summary), including essential questions.

October 4, 1993 (Monday) -- Proposal Meeting for all Faculty (10 minutes per advisor; master lists of topics to be distributed beforehand)

October 8, 1993 (Friday) -- Proposal for members of Exhibition Committee with Letters of Invitation

October 11, 1993 -- Upper School Faculty Meeting to comfirm Exhibition Committees

***October 12 - 29, 1993 -- Introductory Meetings with EC

November 4-8 -- Fall Forum in Louisville, KY

November 12, 1993 (Friday) -- Rough Draft of Senior Thesis Proposal using Essential Question Format due to Advisor

November 15, 1993 (Monday) -- Faculty Meeting to review Proposals

December 1, 1993 -- Post-Graduate Plan and College Essays and Applications due. **Preliminary Proposal for Non-Written Component of Autobiography due to advisor.**

December 13 -17, 1993 -- Week of Mid-Terms

<u>1994</u>

January 3, 1994 -- Autobiographic Portfolio (All six pieces.)

January 14, 1994 -- Last date to resubmit unacceptable portfolios

February 18, 1994 -- Annotated Bibliography due.

February 28-March 4, 1994 -- WINTERIM

March 14, 1994 -- First Draft of Written Component due

March 28, 1994 -- Second Drafts due

April 1-11, 1994 -- SPRING BREAK

April 15, 1994 -- Final Drafts of Senior Thesis Due (5 copies for EC)

April 18-27, 1994 -- Rehearsals for presentations

April 28-30, 1994 -- Senior Thesis Symposium

May 2-11, 1994 -- Evaluative Exit Interviews with EC

June -- Commencement

Not only did Heathwood Hall graduate its Seniors by Exhibition publicly in the spring of 1994, but the staff — to its credit — assembled 6 weeks later to review and revise the entire system! As mentioned earlier, the need to critically review performance assessments, to look at "what worked" and "what didn't," to be willing to make continual progress in developing those Exhibitions which will best reflect what students know and can do, is an essential ingredient in the performance assessment process. Despite all the time spent creating the original *Senior Exhibitions Handbook*, the Heathwood Hall community understood the need to look at "what happened" while the student performances were still fresh in their minds (even though there were videotapes). After reviewing the *Senior Exhibition Handbook,* we will critically evaluate it and consider what areas the Heathwood Hall staff believed needed improvement for the 1995 Exhibitions.

TEMPERED SUCCESS: A GOOD START, THE DESIRE TO IMPROVE

The Senior Exhibitions were an exciting public event in the Heathwood Hall community. Students had met the deadlines, prepared their portfolios, written their theses, and presented their orals to supportive audiences. The *Handbook* had proven utilitarian, and the staff's guidance had helped students initiate a new system for the school. Reviewing the *Handbook*, we can see the strong foundation which undergirds the Senior Exhibition. After critically examining the *Handbook*, the issues which the staff believed needed reconsideration will be reviewed.

The lucid philosophical statement which opens the *Senior Exhibitions Handbook* articulates Heathwood Hall's commitment to the Coalition of Essential School's Nine Common Principles, translated appropriately for Heathwood's student body. The **Habits of Hearts and Mind** section portrays the desired outcomes in clear yet general terms. The description of **The Autobiographic Portfolio** focuses students on Essential Questions and then clearly delineates the six required elements of the Portfolio. Note how each requirement is detailed so that students can be clear as to the expectations. And, as with so many Exhibitions already studied, there is premium put on student reflection throughout the Autobiographic section. The clearly articulated rubric is another feature which links this Exhibition to others and helps contributes to student success.

The description of the **Senior Thesis** not only clearly focuses students on their tasks, but also presents students with a sense of what their public symposium will be like. Because students work closely with faculty members throughout this process, they are guided so their work will, in fact, have a clear "intellectual focus" with demonstrated "sustained and substantive research," as well as the other features required for graduation. The detailed rubric reinforces both expectations and goals. In all, the *Handbook* provides an excellent template for developing a Senior graduation-by-exhibition program. Nonetheless, this was the first Senior Exhibition at Heathwood Hall, and the staff understood the need to critically reflect on the experience.

While generally pleased with the student performances, there was a sense that these initial Exhibitions did not have the depth of intellectual rigor the staff desired. This is not an uncommon phenomena in the early stages of performance assessment implementation. Did these Exhibitions represent enough facets of student mastery? Did the enthusiasm teachers had for their students' *willingness* to tackle these first Exhibitions interfere with the "cool" judgment needed to critically evaluate performances? (*See* Joseph McDonald's *Anatomy of an Exhibition: Warm, Cool, and Hard*, Coalition of Essential School's Exhibitions Collection publication, Providence, RI 02912) And what of some of the logistical problems? Students had traditionally written wonderful autobiographies in the senior year Language Arts class. Should they duplicate much of that work in the *Autobiographic Portfolio?*

The Heathwood Hall faculty raised these questions and more. Despite the community support and acclaim for the Senior Exhibitions, despite their own pride in the accomplishments of their students, the staff willingly put themselves under the microscope so as to improve *next year's* Exhibitions. So, while their first attempt was a very good one, their own expectation is that the next round will be even better. Consider how important this is to improving curriculum and instruction for a school — and how difficult. Breaking the norms of teacher isolation, changing the focus of an entire assessment system, developing a publicly accountable graduation system — any one of these characteristics would be a tall order. It requires a genuine commitment to a shared vision for a faculty, any faculty, to willingly engage in restructuring and transformation at this level.

Heathwood Hall's faculty made the commitment to their philosophical statement, designed and implemented a performance assessment system, and continues to reflect on their work. The Senior Exhibition at Heathwood Hall, with all its attendant features, provides a fine example of ongoing work *from the field* — work which requires vision and commitment, but work which bears tremendous potential for all of our students.

COMMON THREADS — LEARNING FROM EXAMPLES

In reviewing the examples from this chapter, what common exhibition characteristics emerge? Most noticeably, students are required to take responsibility for their work. The element of public presentation also figures prominently in the examples. Multitasked designs, requiring students to present work in a variety of modes, appears again and again. Known outcomes, scoring rubrics, and teacher-coaching are also recurring features in these examples. *Required* student reflection is another regular feature of the exhibitions, aimed at developing an important *habit* in students.

As with other performance assessments, exhibitions require a rethinking of curriculum and instruction. Because exhibitions are culminating projects, presented at the end of a quarter, semester, or school year, they cast a shadow back on the *entire* curriculum. If students will have to demonstrate a variety of skills and attitudes to successfully complete an exhibition, if they are to present what they know about content studied, then the coursework **leading up to** the exhibition must be designed to meet the exhibition's requirements and standards. It is "teaching to a (new) test," in a new fashion. Because the goals are known, the standards are set, the criteria are published, and the expectations are articulated, exhibitions become a key factor in transforming and restructuring curriculum, instruction, and schools. They require long and serious discussions *before* any designing commences. They require public inclusion and education, willingly submitting exhibition ideas to the criticisms, skepticism, and concerns of the community. Input from students should be elicited, too.

This is no minor task — exhibitions are *big* projects requiring careful design and deep thought. They are focused on outcomes, and on students' achieving those outcomes, no matter what. Commitment to exhibitions should only come after teachers and administrators, students, and the community, have begun to implement other performance assessments with their appropriate teaching strategies. But the rewards are great and, more important, clearly point toward public accountability for high standards. Exhibitions are the culmination of an performance assessment *process* which can radically improve curriculum and instruction, which can increase public awareness of what students know and are able to do, and can help teachers more accurately gauge the effectiveness of their programs.

As with the other performance assessments, exhibitions face resistance, apprehension, and skepticism. They require risk-takers firmly grounded in student-centered philosophy and constructivist theory. And they generate engagement, excitement, and enthusiasm among students and the community. They are the logical end-point to an performance assessment system, providing the final evidence that students have progressed and achieved. They are the *mileposts* by which students and teachers can evaluate the measure of their work and the efficacy of their programs. They are the landmarks which we aim for on the horizons of the territory ahead.

4

STANDARDS, CRITERIA, AND RUBRICS: INCLUDING TEACHERS AND STUDENTS IN THE SEARCH FOR QUALITY

> **standard:** An acknowledged measure of comparison for quantitative or qualitative value; A degree or level of requirement, excellence, or attainment.
>
> *The American Heritage Dictionary*

The nation is rife with arguments and debates over *standards*. Every professional organization representing teachers in each discrete discipline has, or is in the process of, churning out *standards* for class-room practitioners. National panels, state commissions, union representatives, and self-appointed "experts" are all presenting the public with *standards*. Is it sound and fury signifying nothing — or is this an important conversation which teachers *need to be a part of*?

The fact is, practicing teachers and their students are seldom invited to join these conversations, much less to serve on the boards, panels, or commissions which ultimately issue *the* "standards." We are left with a melange of ideas, concepts, prescriptions, and possible requirements which will be foisted on those who have had the least input, but potentially possess, along with local parents, the most knowledge about the issue.

And, amidst all the hew and cry about *standards,* the issue of quality seldom surfaces. When these organizations present their standards, are they telling us these are standards of excellence or merely "acceptable" standards? All of this has implications for teachers and students, of course, and is inextricably woven into the concept of performance assessment. Because performance assessments are ultimately geared toward *performance*, teachers and students must be **totally clear** as to what performance standards for excellence, acceptability, or reworking are.

The history and legacy of testing in this country is one of internally subjective and externally arbitrary evaluation of student work. Do any two teachers in the *same* department in the *same* school give *the same* "B" or "A?" If not, what is an "A" or "B" in that school worth? What is the *standard* for "A" or "B" work? And who decides? And by what process? And how does the student know? These are important questions which are seldom raised. Because so much, in terms of student "success," is determined by external test results (SATs, Regents exams, Metropolitan Reading exams, etc.), no culture has emerged in schools about standards or quality. It is only in the last decade, since the school restructuring movement has gained momentum, that discussions about standards and quality have become issues for debate. That debate, however, has been controlled by external agencies, often far from the classroom. In moving to performance assessments, teachers can, and must, bring the discussion about standards and quality to the forefront in their schools. As with so many issues present in the world of the '90s, the standards and quality debate is one in which *teachers and students* can think globally and act locally, with genuine impact.

The inherent problems revolving around the standards issue as it exists today are these:

- ♦ What is the purpose for setting standards — and who makes that decision?
- ♦ Where does the question of quality emerge in the standards debate — and how will that conversation be framed?
- ♦ How do parents and students know what the standards are in their school — and how are those standards implemented?

Before specifically discussing standards, anyone involved in such a conversation must be clear as to what "standards" truly represent. Ultimately, "standards" are about ***accountability***. They create the yardstick by which we measure the accomplishment of our students and our educational programs. Have we met the "standards" of the State, of ETS, and so on? The primary problem with the current system is that the standards by which schools and students are measured are detached and arbitrary systems inflicted upon the local community. The strongest advocates for performance assessments have made compelling arguments enumerating the changes which need to occur if we are to develop systems which are genuinely *accountable,* with clear and known standards where they will have the greatest impact — in the individual classrooms and schools of this nation. The challenge to develop local standards which focus on *the quality of student work,* then, is one of the key aspects of developing an performance assessment system. As with so much of the work with performance assessments, this requires a radical shift in school norms.

DEVELOPING LOCAL STANDARDS FOR QUALITY STUDENT WORK

Several embedded norms have to shift if we are to develop useful and credible standards and systems of genuine accountability in schools.

♦ Teacher isolation, working in cellular classrooms and having little contact or conversation with other teachers, must stop.

♦ Administrators must become *facilitators of opportunity* to insure that teachers have common time to meet around meaningful agendas which focus on student work.

♦ School boards and communities, administrators and teachers, must publicly discuss the **meaning** of standardized tests and seriously consider whether these instruments provide **useful feedback** about authentic teaching and learning in their community.

♦ Students must be invited to join these conversations to learn to reflect on the *meaning* of their schooling. This has to "make sense" to the students or it will simply be another exercise in which the adults of the community impose mandates and structures on students, resulting in young people going through motions which make little or no sense to them.

Crucial to all these conversations is clearly understanding what it is we want our students to leave our school systems with. So, not only must we be clear about what it is we want our students to know and be able to do, but we must also be equally clear about what the standards are for achievement. And those standards must then serve as the accountability measure for our schools.

In *Assessing Student Performance* (Jossey-Bass, 1993), Grant Wiggins has made a strong case for implementing performance assessment systems which build *accountability* into their standards for achievement. In no uncertain tones, Wiggins characterizes the present system this way:

> Too many teachers and administrators are in the habit of accepting praise for student success while explaining why student failure is not their fault. . . . In the absence of an accountability system that would make teachers worry more about the effects of their teaching than the intent, many educators still do not understand their jobs: many wrongly come to think that their purpose is to teach what they know and like, on a relatively fixed schedule — *irrespective of the*

learning that does or does not ensue. . . . In short, teachers are not now obligated, either by job description or direct pressures on the institution by other institutions, to *really* know how they are doing and to do something about it when things go badly.

Assessing Student Performance, p. 276

It is important to note here that Wiggins is not teacher-bashing. He is effectively describing the culture which exists in most schools. In the absence of clearly defined local standards which schools and teachers are held accountable to, educators consistently mistake intent for effect. And this is the point at which performance assessment implementation *has to* attack the existing norms of schools, bringing about authentic change aimed at producing quality student work geared toward high standards.

In *Graduation by Exhibition* (ASCD, 1993), Joseph McDonald states, "Schools wrestling with standards typically begin by building internal mechanisms for teachers to talk with one another about the quality of student work"(p. 55). This starting point speaks to the first changed norm which *must* occur if we are do develop meaningful standards in our schools. Wiggins likens it to a coaching staff whose team is 0 and 6 at midseason. Because their goals are known, because standards of (athletic) performance are clear, such a staff would *have to* reassess its approach and make adjustments so the team's success would improve (*Assessing Student Performance,* p. 277). Nothing like this occurs in schools today because teachers — even teachers in the same department — have little or no idea what anyone else does, much less what the quality of student work is! As Wiggins points out "How many middle schools require that their faculty spend a day with high school faculty to learn how well or poorly their former students have been prepared?"or "How many high schools organize focus groups of college professors to find out how their syllabi, assignments, and tests are viewed?" (p. 266) The examples, at present, are few and far between. Yet, if we are to establish genuine standards and build in real accountability, such practices *must* begin to emerge. And this is where another norm must change.

Administrators can no longer conceive of schools as hierarchical bureaucracies with a top-down management structure. With the advent of performance assessment systems, it is incumbent upon administrators to become *facilitators of opportunities* for teachers. While sounding the call and providing some vision for higher standards and accountability, administrators must be inventive and creative in finding ways for teachers to meet and discuss what their school's standards are — and how teachers will be held accountable for helping students meet those standards. There **are** ways to do this, even in traditional and rigidly structured schools. "Stealing time" for teachers may be the greatest challenge administrators face in shifting the culture of their schools, but it can be done. Imagine the difference in school culture if faculty meetings were considered Workshops or Work Sessions focused on developing standards, rather than administrative meetings about hall duty and detention? How much of what occurs in most faculty meetings could be accomplished through simple memos to staff, saving valuable time for real work for teachers?

What if periods were shortened by 3–5 minutes each on the day of a faculty meeting, creating an additional half to three-quarters of an hour for teachers to meet to focus on the serious work of developing standards? What if administrators and Guidance Counselors offered to "cover" classes for a group of teachers for half a day, allowing those teachers to meet for discussions about standards and accountability? These are not impossible proposals which "can't happen." Almost any administrator could use these mechanisms and others to find time for teachers to meet to discuss standards in their school.

In the same way, any standards conversation must begin by looking at how we gauge our standards at present. Often, SAT or other external, standardized tests are the only measure. Have people from the community, the school board, and the schools themselves ever sat down and discussed whether this is a useful measure of student achievement? Are these the standards to which we hold our students? Since students never know which questions they got right or wrong, how can a culture of student progress toward the achievement of standards be created around such measures? If these conversations are not broached, it is unlikely any school can develop authentic standards or provide suitable accountability for its work.

And what of the students themselves? At present, students have little or no voice or choice in schools. This is not to say, as was characterized to me by a colleague once, that we need to "turn the asylum over to the inmates," but to ask whether teachers are, in fact, coordinating intent and effect. As Wiggins cogently notes:

> We are still light-years away from treating students as clients seeking a service — clients who are able to seek and receive change in the (daily) service when the methods used and prescriptions made by teachers fail to help them. . . . It is almost unheard of for teachers to have their ineffective methods challenged, their questionable grades overturned, or their classroom duties altered because of a failure to serve the clients well. . . . The voice option is the only way in which dissatisfied customers or members can react. . . .
>
> *Assessing Student Performance*, p. 263

His proposals for creating greater student voice may seem radical, but they are simply outside the bounds of the present norms. If we are to begin to engage in serious conversations about developing standards and systems of accountability which are genuinely effective, we might do well to consider Wiggins's ideas.

> The primary "unit" of accountability is the *particular* set of teachers and administrators that are *directly* responsible for each child's experience and achievement. . . . Schools would thus be instantly more accountable if we worried less about arcane psychometric proxy tests and worried more about making the teacher's daily work public and giving the student performer a more powerful voice. . . . . What if each teacher had to display monthly the best work from *each* student in a public place in school? . . . What if performance appraisals were centered on teacher self-assessment in reference to a range of student work from a major assignment? These are the kinds of mechanisms which would improve accountability immediately and force-fully.
>
> *Assessing Student Performance*, p. 264

While these suggestions depart from present practice, consider how they bring together the "norm-breaking" which is proposed here. Teachers participating in this type of system would *have to* talk to each other about the student work and range of assignments displayed. Administrators would *have to* facilitate the creation of an atmosphere where teachers would be *encouraged and rewarded* for participating. Students would gain a powerful voice in a public forum, being able to examine their work next to others, as well as examine the work of their teachers, engendering conversations about "what works" and "what doesn't," thereby improving the quality of the educational program. Most significantly, this entire approach makes public the issue of standards and accountability — thereby helping everyone focus on what is most important about teaching and learning, the student's progress.

This is not a discussion about "Standards — How To." It is a provocation for teachers, students, administrators, parents, and school boards. What *are* your standards? How are they determined and how do they, in turn, determine accountability for students and teachers? The suggestions here call for a new way to approach the issue; a way which defies the norms which currently exist in most schools. Giving greater voice to those closest to the work — the students and teachers — and asking other members of the Learning Community to enter the conversation — these suggestions represent an outline of how to *begin* the conversation. At present, schools have no standards. The variance of what a grade is worth from one classroom to the next is mind boggling. Until the serious conversations begin, until teachers are given the time to meet and talk, until parents and administrators support and facilitate these conversations, and until students are consulted as part of the process, we will continue to swim in very murky waters arbitrarily labeled "standards." This is a process, not an event, and it is a process which is a logical and integral part of developing a performance assessment system. For the classroom teacher, an entry point which is equally significant to performance assessments and easily accessible to classroom practice, is criteria and rubrics.

DEVELOPING RUBRICS AND SCORING CRITERIA
TO DEFINE STANDARDS

Rubric: Any brief, authoritative rule or direction.
Criterion: A standard, rule, or test on which a judgment
or decision can be based.

The American Heritage Dictionary

Translating standards into classroom application can occur
through the development and use of rubrics and scoring criteria.
In its ecclesiastical definition, a "rubric" was a direction or set of
instructions, generally printed in red (its meaning in Latin), explaining how liturgical services were to be rendered. In essence, rubrics
were instructions or guidelines which explained how a performance
should be properly presented. In classroom terms, a rubric is a guideline for determining how well students are performing any number
of tasks in relation to the standards of the school. It is, most common-
ly, a scoring device which allows a judge (a teacher or other audience)
to distinguish how effectively students are performing assigned
tasks.

Criteria are those descriptors or indicators which clarify for
both performers and audience what is required to succeed at certain
tasks. For example, the criteria for pole-vaulting involves, first and
foremost, clearing the crossbar without knocking it off the stanchions.
Other criteria might describe mechanical procedures, like how the
pole should be held, the length of the approach track, the speed
recommended for the vaulter, the proper placement of the pole
on the ground, and so on. Criteria, in Grant Wiggins's words, "involve the conditions that any performance must meet to be successful; they define, operationally, what meeting the task requirements
means" ("What is a Rubric?" **C.L.A.S.S.** document, 1994, p. 3). So,
one criterion for hitting a home run in baseball is that the ball must
clear the fence in fair territory between the left field and right field
foul poles.

Here we begin to see where rubrics and standards intersect with
the notion of criteria. A Little League home run will greatly differ
from one hit at Yankee Stadium — but the criteria remains the same.
The standard is *equivalent*, though **not** equal — the performer must
be able to achieve a feat which requires uncommon strength and

timing. The *ultimate* standard of excellence and achievement might be hitting the ball out of Yankee Stadium, but we adjust our standards and rubrics so that performers from novice through expert levels can be judged as to how well they meet the criteria *at their level*.

To use a more academic example: students are capable of identifying **excellent** writing. If asked, they can bring in an example of writing they believe is excellent and they can defend it. In that defense, they will identify characteristics — indicators — of excellent writing. Many of these will be basic criteria which apply to *any* writing, no matter what level the performer is at. Very often students (and teachers) identify writing criteria related to *mechanics, organization, content, sentence structure,* and *vocabulary.* Certainly, these are important criteria for writing, but they speak to one of the most significant problems which surrounds the standards–rubric–criteria discussion. That is, do any of the listed writing criteria reflect any aspect of the *quality* of the writing being judged? In other words, a totally bland, uninteresting, poorly documented piece of writing could, in fact, score fairly well if those were the only criteria used. *This is where our search for standards intersects with rubrics and scoring criteria and opens the door for classroom teachers to begin these conversations with their students.*

TEASING OUT QUALITY THROUGH RUBRIC DESIGN

Throughout the earlier chapters, examples of performance assessments often included rubrics and scoring criteria — and statements were made as to how those rubrics and criteria were, in some way, flawed. The remainder of this chapter will be aimed at presenting rubrics and criteria to analyze the strengths and weaknesses in what we present as guidelines to student performance. Embedded in such analysis is the question of standards and quality. As has been mentioned before, even if the rubrics and scoring criteria accompanying a performance assessment are not "perfect," they are still a marked improvement over what has gone before — students working in a total vacuum regarding what the expectations for quality work might be other than an individual teacher's subjective, idiosyncratic judgment.

What follows then, is a careful look at three examples of rubrics and scoring criteria to see what we can learn about standards and quality and how we can best develop meaningful instruments to evaluate student work. The format for each investigation is the same: we consider *"what works," "what doesn't,"* and what are the *implications for standards and quality.* Between the examples and the discussion of each, some sense of how one might develop a comparable system for classrooms should emerge.

THE PIERRE VAN CORTLANDT MIDDLE SCHOOL NEWSPAPER PROJECT

WHAT WORKS

Rick Casey's newspaper project for middle schoolers in Croton-on-Hudson, New York, makes it clear that **Work Habits, Research,** and **Presentation** (Fig. 4.1) are the focus of the assessment. Within those categories we can tease out the important standards:

- ◆ Meeting deadlines; using class time effectively.
- ◆ Thorough research of content.
- ◆ Attention to detail regarding writing mechanics and appearance.

If you were a middle schooler engaged in this project, it should be clear to you what the expectations for success are.

WHAT DOESN'T

As with so many first-generation rubrics and scoring criteria, the focus of attention here is on mechanics, observation of student industry, and "good citizenship" (meeting deadlines). It is difficult to nail down what we consider *high quality* work in written terms and, in fact, until student work is collected and examined, students cannot be presented with clear examples of what we mean. As mentioned earlier, students could achieve "E" ratings for their work on this project *without* producing a newspaper which was particularly interesting to read! It could have all the facts right, all deadlines met, and it could *look* wonderful (thanks to students knowing how to manipulate a good graphics software program) *without* achieving a level of writing which was memorable, or engaging, or of particularly good quality.

FIGURE 4.1: VAN CORTLANDT MIDDLE SCHOOL —
NEWSPAPER PROJECT GRADING CRITERIA

American Revolutionary Newspaper
Grading Criteria

Although you may elect to complete this project working in a group of 1-3 students. each student will be graded individually. Students will receive separate grades for each of the criteria below:

Work Habits
Students will be given a considerable amount of class time for research, drafting and word processing of information.   In order to ensure that students do not fall behind in their work, they will have to produce one finalized written piece every other day.

    E - Student meets all deadlines: observation indicates that student consistently uses class
        time toward completion of this assignment.
    G - Student fails to meet 1-2 deadlines, but shows consistent. daily progress toward
        completion of this project. Student consistently uses class time toward completion
        of the assignment.
    S - Student fails to meet 1-2 deadlines. Progress is inconsistent. but noticeable.
        Student uses class time only when directed to do so.
    N - Student fails to meet 3 or more deadlines. Student fails to complete all required parts
        of the newspaper. Student fails to use class time despite teacher prompting.

Research
Each of the 7 pieces of this assignment should show student research into the events of the American Revolutionary period.

    E - Articles indicate a thorough and accurate understanding of the events and issues of the
        Revolutionary era. No gaps or misstatements in content are noted.
    G - Articles indicate a clear grasp of the events and issues of the period. however, some
        minor gaps or misstatements are noted.
    S - Articles indicate only a cursory or superficial understanding of the events and
        issues being reported. Some serious gaps a/o misstatements are noted.
    N - Articles indicate no understanding of the issues and events of the period.
        Articles lack important information a/o contain numerous misstatements of fact.

Presentation
Newspapers should be pleasing to the eye. and be "reader-friendly". Articles should be proofread and be free of spelling, grammatical and mechanical errors. Articles continued on another page should be clearly marked.

    E - Newspaper shows careful planning and a consistent format. Graphics are included.
        Newspaper has obviously been proofread for errors. All components, including
        headlines, by-lines and datelines are noted. All requirements are met.
    G - Articles are generally free of spelling and grammatical errors. All components are
        noted. All requirements are met. Graphics are included.
    S - Articles are generally free of spelling and grammatical errors. One or more components
        have been omitted. One or two requirements have not been met. Graphics are
        included.
    N - Articles contain numerous spelling and grammatical errors. Layout is inconsistent.
        Numerous components are missing. More than two requirements are missing.
        No graphics are included.

IMPLICATIONS FOR STANDARDS AND QUALITY

The obvious implication regarding this grading criteria is that the next generation of it needs to pay more attention to quality — particularly regarding writing. Because examples would now exist (those newspapers produced by this group), teachers and students will be able to identify what quality writing for this project might be and the rubric can be revised accordingly. The conversation students and teachers have about that revision is the most important implication regarding the development of standards.

THE FULTON VALLEY PREP/PINER HIGH SCHOOL SCIENCE FAIR RUBRIC

WHAT WORKS

First and foremost, the classifications of **Mastery** and **Distinguished** indicate levels of achievement for which students should aspire (Fig. 4.2). In that sense, the message sent to students is that nothing less is really acceptable and that students are being held to high expectations. The rubric is clear in its requirements:

♦ Students are expected to show their *process* of development.

♦ A substantial *amount* of work is expected to be placed on display.

♦ Attention to an understanding of Newtonian Physics is expected.

♦ There is a definite value on group cooperation stressed.

WHAT DOESN'T

One of the most difficult problems with developing rubrics and scoring criteria is **language**. While terms might be explained and discussed, with examples, in class, questions still arise as to the real *meaning* of terms used in a rubric like this. What is "striking" or "attractive?" *How much* "attention to detail" is "careful?" What does an "in-depth summary" look like compared to one without depth? In the same way, *how* do conclusions reveal "thoughtful and significant insight?"

FIGURE 4.2: FULTON VALLEY PREP/PINER HIGH SCHOOL — SCIENCE FAIR RUBRIC

Fulton
Valley
Prep

Sciences Core
The Physics of Sports and Recreation

Rubric for Science Fair Projects

Mastery:	Distinguished:
1. Display Board clearly reflects the product development process.	**Overall:** Display Board is striking, attractive, well-organized, thorough and shows careful attention to detail.
2. Display Board includes summaries of all experiments and the results, with appropriate illustrations, measurements, calculations, and graphs.	1. See *Mastery*.
3. Display Board includes a model or drawing of the final product.	2. See *Mastery*. Also, neatly written, thorough, in-depth summaries of experiments, including quantative data, measurements, calculations and graphs.
4. Display Board includes writeup with appropriate conclusions based on data.	3. See *Mastery*. Also, model or drawing is to scale, neat, clearly labelled, and detailed.
5. Display Board includes thorough explanation of the relevance of the principles of Newtonian physics to the performance of the product.	4. See *Mastery*. Also, conclusions show thoughtful and significant insight into the experimental results and data.
6. Notebook is a thorough record of the process of the development of the final product, including **lab writeups, answers to assigned questions, vocabulary exercises, and reflective writings** about the concepts, experiments and results.	5. See *Mastery*. Also shows clear connections between the performance of the product and the Newtonian principles involved.
7. Product exhibits care in thought, planning, and construction. Attention to detail is evident.	6. See *Mastery*. Notebook entries are thoughtful and in-depth and reflect clear insight into the connections between the experiments, readings, and concepts.
	7. See *Mastery*. Product also shows originality and creativity.

It is easy to pick on the vocabulary used in a rubric or scoring criteria, but it is a highly significant point to focus on. Again, without examples of prior student work — whether in writing or on video- or audiotape, or in some other medium — it is extremely difficult for students to know what we mean when we use terms like these.

IMPLICATIONS

One possible solution, or at least a strategy, is to present students with a rubric like this, conduct a discussion *about the terms in question*, and record the examples which arise *from the class*. Those examples then become **part** of the final rubric which students will use in developing their projects. In this way, the scoring criteria becomes more clear to the students, and the standards which we are aiming for begin to flesh themselves out for students and teachers.

The Fulton Valley Prep example is a good one to include among our models because it presents an uncompromising approach to the *level of achievement* we can set for our students. While we must always gauge whether our students are ready for Yankee Stadium, it never hurts to consider setting the crossbar at a challenging height and demanding the stretch for excellence, while always building a safety net for repeated attempts at improvement.

FULTON VALLEY PREP/PINER HIGH SCHOOL HEROES EXHIBITION RUBRIC

WHAT WORKS

The refinement of the Science Fair rubric we witness here, is the creation of categories for "Project Content," "Project Format," and "Defense" (Fig. 4.3). Again, consider what this *immediately* tells students — there is an expectation regarding content, there is a standard regarding format, there *will be* an oral defense of the project. There are some basic expectations articulated in the rubric as well: a research component including a bibliography; a written presentation based on a proscribed format; neatness, graphics, and a variety of presentational modes; an oral component which encourages well-rehearsed and articulate presentation, ready to field questions about the work.

FIGURE 4.3: FULTON VALLEY PREP/PINER HIGH SCHOOL—
HEROES EXHIBITION RUBRIC

HEROES Exhibition
A Collection of Heroes
Rubric

	Mastery (B)	Distinguished (A)
PROJECT CONTENT	1. The project contains a clear, thoughtful definition of a hero for our society.	1. The project contains a clear, thoughtful, multi-faceted definition of a hero for our society.
	2. The project includes a collection of heroes who fit the author's definition.	2. The project includes a varied collection of heroes who fit the author's definition.
	3. Each hero in the collection is described accurately and connections between the heroes and the definition are evident.	3. Each hero in the collection is described accurately and in detail and connections between the heroes and the definition are clearly drawn .
	4. The author has researched the heroes in the collection and has included a bibliography of sources.	4. The author has thoroughly researched the heroes in the collection and has included a bibliography of sources.

Note: *The size of the collection (number of heroes) should be related both to the choice of format and the depth of descriptions. E.g. a calendar would show 12 heroes and trading cards probably 12-15, while a speech or monologue series would present 3-4 heroes in greater depth.*

PROJECT FORMAT	1. Written material is the original creation of the author or is clearly labeled as a quotation with the source identified. 2. Written materials are organized and readable, with an introduction, body and conclusion. Hypercard stacks allow easy travel among cards. 3. Written materials are neatly hand-written in ink or typed and contain few spelling, punctuation or usage errors. 4. The layout and graphics in an anthology, calendar, cards, magazine or mural are neat and easy to follow. 5. The performer (series of monologues or speech) speaks clearly and loudly and, although using a script, shows evidence of ample rehearsal.	1. Written material is the original creation of the author or is clearly labeled as a quotation with the source identified. 2. Written materials are well-organized and interesting, with an introduction, body and conclusion. Hypercard stacks allow easy travel among cards and use graphics and backgrounds creatively. 3. Written materials are typed and contain minimal spelling, punctuation or usage errors. 4. The layout and graphics in an anthology, calendar, cards, magazine or mural are creative, eye-catching and professional-looking. 5. The performer (series of monologues or speech) speaks clearly and loudly and has memorized the material, referring minimally to note cards. The presentation is energetic, believable and convincing.
DEFENSE	1. The presenter can explain reasons for his/her definition and can field questions about the heroes in the collection.	1. The presenter can explain connections between his/her definition and our society and can thoroughly defend her/his choice of heroes for the collection.

WHAT DOESN'T

In general this is an effective rubric which suffers from the same problems as the earlier ones — terminology and the question of quality. And, again, in the absence of specific examples of student work, it might be hard for students to understand what constitutes a product which is "creative, eye-catching, and professional-looking."

Once again the issue of quality has to be raised, too. If the expectation is "professional-looking" work, should it be compared to a magazine we purchase on a newsstand? If so, then which one? What is the baseline for quality here? Is it previous student work — that is, earlier work by these particular students, or work done by students from previous classes?

IMPLICATIONS

The problem raised by the quality issue is the difficult one and speaks directly to the standards question. On what basis are we gauging the quality of our students' work? What are the benchmarks? What are the "anchors" of high quality (a Grant Wiggins term) against which student *know* their work will be judged? What will the assessors use to compare this work to? What is fair, yet still high quality? How much weight do we give to the *progress* students have made since they began the class? Do we consider *effort*, even if the quality is poor? These are not simple questions to answer and this is not meant to denigrate the Fulton Valley Prep work. Again, we are looking at first-generation attempts at establishing standards and making evaluation clear to students. In this case, we have a school which has begun a process which will reap greater rewards each year it continues to work on clarifying the rubrics and scoring criteria which accompany their performance assessments. In and of itself, this is a vast improvement in our efforts to know better what our students truly know and are able to do — and it serves them better in achieving outcomes of significance which will pay dividends in the future.

THE JOEL BARLOW WRITING RUBRICS: PROGRESS THROUGH PROCESS

Joel Barlow High School in West Redding, Connecticut, has been developing its Junior Writing Portfolio for a number of years.

In that time, the teachers involved in the project have continuously refined their work. Theirs is an excellent model on two levels: the quality of the rubrics developed for students to improve their writing with and the well-organized *process* of that rubric development by the staff. It is worth departing from the "What Works," "What Doesn't" format to carefully examine each piece of the Barlow system. There are five elements which distinguish the work at Barlow: Clarity, Diagnosis, Definitions, Exemplars, and Staff Self-Reflection.

CLARITY

The Barlow system goes to great lengths to establish clarity. First, there is a description of "Rubric Levels" (Fig. 4.4). This establishes a six-point rating scale ranging from "exemplary" to "errors block meaning." This format *clearly* establishes the format with which all writing for the junior portfolio will be evaluated. As with earlier examples, this model suffers from some language problems (what is "sophisticated" writing, for example), **but** those problems are compensated for in two ways: the creation of a Narrative Writing Rubric, and a worksheet designed to clarify "Qualities of Good Writing." So, while we may not *initially* be clear about what "sophisticated" writing is, these two supporting documents greatly clarify the task for the students and the teachers. And, as with those rubrics which are most effective, this model provides a statement about standards with a clear delineation of criteria. For those wrestling with developing a standards, criteria, rubric system, the Joel Barlow example presents an excellent process model — particularly notable because its first concern is *clarity*.

(Text continues on page 139.)

FIGURE 4.4: JOEL BARLOW HIGH SCHOOL — WRITING RUBRICS

| RUBRIC LEVELS |
| Descriptions |

6   EXEMPLARY
The writing is sophisticated, complex, skillful, artful, rich, and shows variety. The use of conventions furthers the meaning and there are no errors.

5   COMMENDABLE
The writing is clear, interesting, appropriate, and generally rich and sophisticated. There are few errors.

4   EFFECTIVE BUT FLAWED
The writing has minor flaws, but is effective. It is acceptable, adequate, generally correct and errors do not interfere with meaning.

3   APPROACHES EFFECTIVE
The writing has serious flaws that interfere with meaning. It is awkward, artificial, limited. Errors interfere with meaning, some sense of conventions but simplistic.

2   POOR
The writing is incomplete or has major flaws. It is poor, lacking parts, insufficient, inappropriate, repetitive, simplistic. It has many errors that interfere with meaning and little sense of conventions.

1   ERRORS BLOCK MEANING
The writing is very limited, inappropriate, meaningless and demonstrates no sense of conventions. The writer is unable to begin effectively.

QUALITIES OF GOOD WRITING

MECHANICS
spelling, punctuation,
capitalization and paragraphing

LANGUAGE
effective variety

SENTENCE STRUCTURE
variety and quality of sentences

CONTENT
supporting details

ORGANIZATION
clarity and logic

THINKING
development of ideas

TASK
writer's choice of voice,
audience, form and purpose

Narrative JBHS Writing Rubric

Directions: Read the piece of writing holistically and give a single holistic score on a six point scale ("6" is exemplary and "1" is very poor). In determining that single score judge the quality of the piece of writing as a whole, giving greater weight to longer and more substantive pieces and rewarding variety and creativity.

6 - A piece of writing that is <u>exemplary</u> in overall quality. It is characteristically substantial in content and mature in style. It demonstrates an ability to use language creatively and effectively. Voice is strong and there is a sophisticated sense of audience, task and choice of form. The writer demonstrates insight, synthesizing complex ideas and generating original ideas. The organization is clear and artful. The content, sentence structure and word choice are rich and sophisticated. The use of mechanics furthers the meaning.

5 - A piece of writing that is <u>commendable</u> in overall quality. It suggests the excellence that a "6" demonstrates, but is less developed, less creative or takes fewer risks. The writing is clear, interesting, appropriate and generally rich and sophisticated. It demonstrates an effective use of voice, details and language. There are few errors in mechanics, usage or sentence structure.

4 - A piece of writing that is <u>effective, but flawed</u> in overall quality. The writing has minor flaws, but is effective. There is a sense of audience and task and appropriate use of form, but some of the writing may seem formulaic. There is some insight, but tends to demonstrate minimal risk taking and original thinking. It is acceptable, generally correct and the errors do not interfere with the meaning.

3 - A piece of writing that <u>approaches effective</u> in overall quality. The writing has flaws that interfere with meaning. The pieces may be too brief or underdeveloped. The writing shows awareness of task, audience and writing conventions but is often awkward or simplistic. There are attempts at analysis but little insight or originality.

2 - A piece of writing that is <u>poor</u> in overall quality. The writing is incomplete or has major flaws. The piece may be either too short and undeveloped or abstract and vague. The writing demonstrates a poor sense of audience and task and no variety. Details are either repetitive or missing. It has many errors that interfere with meaning and little sense of conventions.

1 - A piece of writing assesed as <u>errors block meaning</u>. There are many weaknesses and few, if any, strengths. The piece of writing shows very little time and thought. The writing is very limited, inappropriate, meaningless and/or demonstrates no sense of conventions.

DIAGNOSIS

The "JBHS Diagnostic Writing Rubric" (Fig. 4.5) is, at its simplest level, a synthesis of *all* the Barlow Descriptions, Guides, and Narrative concepts. Its value is in understanding the context of it *in-use*.

To use the Diagnostic Rubric effectively, a rater would *have to be* familiar with each of the Descriptions and Guides. As we consider the *process* of developing a standards, criteria, and rubric system, the importance of collaborative conversation and work around rubric development is crucial. Before reading a single paper and using this Diagnostic Rubric, a rater would had to have engaged in clarifying discussions with other teachers as to what each category and rating item meant. Here we can see how *clarity* contributes to the development of a system which considers *diagnosis* an early, significant component in the writing process.

So, while the descriptions on the Rubric itself are cryptic, the expectation is that rater's have been deeply involved in clarifying and understanding each category of writing skills and each item to be rated. And, of course, rater's can refer to the more detailed descriptions for each category if there is any question about a paper. Again, the *process* which teachers engage in, developing this kind of rubric and system, is what distinguishes the Barlow model.

(Text continues on page 142.)

FIGURE 4.5: JOEL BARLOW HIGH SCHOOL — DIAGNOSTIC WRITING RUBRIC

TASK	THINKING	ORGANIZATION	CONTENT
writer's choice of voice, audience, form and purpose	development of ideas	clarity and logic	supporting details
EXEMPLARY			
skillfully uses variety of voices	synthesizes complex ideas	clearly and artfully ordered	rich and substantive
sophisticated sense of audience	sophisticated evaluation of ideas	organization enhances meaning	stimulates new responses
sees complexities/implications	generates original ideas		
sophisticated choice of form	keen insight		
COMMENDABLE			
effective use of voice	synthesizes ideas	clearly focused	interesting and meaningful
clear sense of audience	careful evaluation of data	skillful transitions	effective use of details
successful execution of task	evidence of original thinking	logical development of ideas	provides "telling" details
effective choice of form	displays insight	effective use of title	
EFFECTIVE BUT FLAWED			
authentic voice	attempts synthesis	generally focused	adequate use of details
sense of audience	evidence of evaluation	consistent point of view	details support focus
purpose stated and achieved	evidence of analysis	organization dominates meaning	provides many details
appropriate use of form	some insight	effective introduction	information correct
		effective conclusion	
APROACHES EFFECTIVE			
artificial or stilted voice	lacks original ideas	focus limited	insufficient detail
some sense of audience	recognizes important data	focus too broad	details don't support focus
some awareness of purpose	attempts analysis	awkward introduction	information generally correct
awkward use of form	little insight	awkward conclusion	
		needs additional transitions	
NOT EFFECTIVE			
little sense of voice	lacks coherence	focus unclear	important details omitted
poor sense of audience	merely recalls data	ineffective introduction	repetitive details
purpose unclear	merely summarizes or tells story	ineffective conclusion	ineffective use of details
predictable response		poorly organized	some incorrect information
poor use of form		lacks transitions	details confusing
ERRORS BLOCK MEANING			
voiceless	not developed	no focus	few details
no sense of audience	provides little data	no introduction	irrelevant details
little or no awareness of purpose		no conclusion	incorrect information
little or no awareness of form		disorganized	

Date: _____   Overall Assessment: _____   Work ev

Comments: _____

SENTENCE STRUCTURE	LANGUAGE	MECHANICS
variety and quality of sentences	effective variety	spelling, punctuation, capitalization and paragraphing
variety enhances style and effect	rich, effective vocabulary	very few or no errors
sophisticated patterns	sophisticated figurative language	use of mechanics futhers meaning
no errors in structure or usage	artful use of dialogue	breaks rules artfully
elegant sentences		
appropriate variety	effective, furthers meaning	few errors
some use of sophisticated structures	generally uses rich language	spelling & capitalization correct
few errors in structure or usage	correct usage	attempts sophisticated punctuation
effective use of syntax	effective figurative language	effective paragraphing
some sentence variety	acceptable vocabulary	errors don't interfere with meaning
attempts sophisticated patterns	attempts sophisticated language	spelling generally correct
errors do not interfere with meaning	generally correct usage	capitalization generally correct
	some figurative language	uses punctuation on a simple level
	effective use of dialogue	generally correct paragraphing
little sentence variety	simple vocabulary	errors interfere with meaning
relies on a few simple patterns	some errors in usage	frequent errors distract
errors interfere with meaning	attempts figurative language	some errors in spelling & capitalization
repetitive structure	attempts dialogue	some errors in punctuation
awkward sentences/syntax		some sense of paragraphing
no sentence variety	simplistic vocabulary	many errors interfere with meaning
uses only simple forms	inappropriate vocabulary	many errors in spelling
errors seriously interfere w/meaning	many errors in usage	many errors in capitalization
		many errors in punctuation
		little sense of paragraphing
no concept of sentence	very limited vocabulary	errors block meaning
		no concept of mechanics
		indecipherable handwriting

aluated: _____

_____ (revised 12/94)

DEFINITIONS

For each major category of concern — Task, Thinking, Organization, Content, Sentence Structure, Language, and Mechanics — the Barlow model provides a *definitions* page (Fig. 4.6) for reference. These definitions are listed on the diagnostic sheet as well, but by having a separate sheet for each, teachers can review with students exactly what the expectations are for each level of work.

Because the language of rubrics can be so problematic, consider how this process can help students be clear about the *definitions* for "exemplary," "commendable," and so on. Imagine, if you will, how this might play out in a classroom situation.

If we are reviewing the "Task" rubric alone, we can see how "Task" itself is defined: "writer's choice of voice, audience, form and purpose." If students have any questions as to what that means, it can be discussed and clarified *before* they begin an assignment. In the same fashion, if a student was not sure what "skillfully uses a variety of voices" means (under Exemplary on the Task rubric) a discussion could ensue — engaging other students in the conversation and making sure the writers have a clear grasp on what it would take to perform a Task in Exemplary fashion.

By breaking each important outcome category down this way, and providing students with clear guidelines for each, the writing process is clarified. This also provides the instructor with an important source of input from students — who is asking what kinds of questions; which words in the descriptors are problematic for the most students; and so on. So, the individual *definitions* is an excellent assessment tool because it provides a **feedback loop** from the moment of its introduction. Not only will it clarify the writing process but it also enables the teachers to acquire important informal feedback about the effectiveness of the rubric before writing begins. In turn, this allows teachers to revisit the rubric to improve for the next group of students. Further clarifying this entire process is *The JBHS Book of Writing Models.*

(Text continues on page 146.)

FIGURE 4.6: JOEL BARLOW HIGH SCHOOL — MODEL DEFINITIONS

> TASK
> writer's choice of voice,
> audience, form and purpose

6 EXEMPLARY
   skillfully uses variety of voices
   sophisticated sense of audience
   sees complexities/implications
   sophisticated choice of form

5 COMMENDABLE
   effective use of voice
   clear sense of audience
   successful execution of task
   effective choice of form

4 EFFECTIVE BUT FLAWED
   authentic voice
   sense of audience
   purpose stated and achieved
   appropriate use of form

3 APPROACHES EFFECTIVE
   artificial or stilted voice
   some sense of audience
   some awareness of purpose
   awkward use of form

2 POOR
   little sense of voice
   poor sense of audience
   purpose unclear
   predictable response
   poor use of form

1 ERRORS BLOCK MEANING
   voiceless
   no sense of audience
   little or no awareness of purpose
   little or no awareness of form

THINKING
development of ideas

---

6 EXEMPLARY
synthesizes complex ideas
sophisticated evaluation of ideas
generates original ideas
keen insight

5 COMMENDABLE
synthesizes ideas
careful evaluation of data
evidence of original thinking
displays insight

4 EFFECTIVE BUT FLAWED
attempts synthesis
evidence of evaluation
evidence of analysis
some insight

3 APPROACHES EFFECTIVE
lacks original ideas
recognizes important data
attempts analysis
little insight

2 POOR
lacks coherence
merely recalls data
merely summarizes or tells story

1 ERRORS BLOCK MEANING
not developed
provides little data

```
┌─────────────────────────────┐
│        ORGANIZATION         │
│       clarity and logic     │
└─────────────────────────────┘
```

6 EXEMPLARY
clearly and artfully ordered
organization enhances meaning

5 COMMENDABLE
clearly focused
skillful transitions
logical development of ideas
effective use of title

4 EFFECTIVE BUT FLAWED
generally focused
consistent point of view
organization diminishes meaning
effective introduction
effective conclusion

3 APPROACHES EFFECTIVE
focus limited
focus too broad
awkward introduction
awkward conclusion
needs additional transitions

2 POOR
focus unclear
ineffective introduction
ineffective conclusion
poorly organized
lacks transitions

1 ERRORS BLOCK MEANING
no focus
disorganized
no introduction
no conclusion

EXEMPLARS

Time and space do not allow for the inclusion of Barlow's "Writing Models" booklet (and it is substantial!). Throughout this chapter and, indeed, throughout this book's discussion of performance assessments, the need for *exemplars* has been mentioned time and again. If students are to truly achieve high standards it serves our best interest to provide them with examples. The Barlow writing program does just that.

The JBHS Book of Writing Models is a wonderful guide for students and teachers, replete with authentic examples of student work representing every item-rating on the scoring rubric! Consider what this means: both students and teachers can examine what an "Exemplary" paper looks like. Discussions can be conducted to tease out each aspect of it: Can we identify why this paper meets the "Exemplary" standard in "Task?" In "Organization?" In "Content?" In the same way, students and teachers can look at papers which are "Commendable" and compare it to "Exemplary," distinguishing where one is stronger or weaker than the other. Imagine how much clearer everyone will be about standards and expectations if this process is used.

The trade-off to accomplish this, of course, is TIME. The fact that the Barlow teachers have worked years to develop this system is important to note. Something like this does not happen overnight. It also means using more time to *include the students* in the process. And this raises a most important point about performance assessments. Because they are more elaborate, more student-inclusive, more complex than traditional assessments, they take more time. We are talking about an important shift in our view of the structure and culture of the school. If good writing is an important outcome, we will need to take the time to develop it. The same process could be applied to various critical thinking and problem solving skills. Taking the time to break down the process, to include the students in the process *so that it has genuine meaning for them,* is not something that happens very often in schools today. Because of an obsession to "cover" content, we *can't* take the TIME to **uncover** the process for our students. Consider what that means. Students never truly understand why they are doing the tasks they are asked to fulfill; they never really "get" writing or history or mathematic problem-solving; they never are clear about why they are following a laboratory "recipe" in science. They go through the motions, they accomplish the task *for the teacher* and a week, or a month, or a year later, have no recollection about the *why* or the process.

The Barlow system is a move away from that mentality. It is designed to engage students in the process of understanding each component of the writing process. It asks them to question, to reflect, to consider each element of their writing and to measure it themselves against exemplary and other models. But this takes TIME. It is raises the hard question for teachers: Will you sacrifice content for process so that students will be able to truly integrate and internalize what they learn? Everyone would agree that we *want* students to integrate and internalize what they learn, but *saying* and *doing* are two different things. The Joel Barlow teachers have taken an ambitious and courageous first step in implementing the *doing*. And, they have also been brave enough to honestly look at the results of their early work with a critical eye, considering what they need to do to improve their system.

STAFF SELF-REFLECTION

After working very hard at developing any performance assessment system, no one is anxious to go back and look at the work critically. Yet, this is an essential component in the assessment process. It is too easy to be pleased with one's work, to be happy to see students *producing* higher quality products, enjoy the energy of greater student engagement. This is not to say that teachers shouldn't be pleased with such work, and shouldn't take some time to congratulate themselves for a job well done. But we have to recognize that the job is incomplete if we do not cast a critical eye on the work. Performance assessment is an incremental, developmental process for students *and* teachers. In essence, the work is never done because each success "ratchets up" our standards and asks us to move the work deeper. The Barlow staff has been willing to accept that challenge.

The "Identified Weaknesses" and "Recommendations to Improve" which are included here (Fig. 4.7), speak to how critically the Joel Barlow teachers take their work, and how honestly they are willing to assess their own progress, not just their students.

FIGURE 4.7: JOEL BARLOW HIGH SCHOOL — STAFF SELF-REFLECTION

Identified Weaknesses of JBHS Writing Portfolios

- Few creative pieces.

- Making meaning is missing.

- A lot of listing.

- Lack of pushing personal narrative to any kind of real analytical level.

- Extraordinary number of mechanical errors that could be cleaned up easily with proof-reading.

- Standard is not being set; rubric calls for it but it is not apparent in the papers.

- Papers show intellectual immaturity but voice spoke of intelligence and alertness and should have been able to push harder.

- Students are paying attention to teachers' grades or content rather than quality of the writing itself.

Recommendations to Improve Process & Portfolio Quality

- Portfolios must be part of classes to improve quantity & quality.

- Students must receive direct instruction in creating a portfolio.

- Students must be provided with the time and response for letters.

- Students must proofread and revise entries carefully.

- Create a portfolio culture at JBHS.

- Assessment has to be turned over into instruction.

Again, this breaks a norm for teachers. In a traditional setting, content is covered, students are tested, grades are issued, and we move on. Occasionally, teachers do item-analysis of tests, or look for recurring problems in writing or problemsolving, but there is no systematic review of the pedagogical and assessment practice. How do we evaluate the strengths and weaknesses of our own curricular programs? Simply keeping a tally sheet on "passes" and "failures" is hardly adequate. What are the strengths of our program; what do we see students *exhibiting* genuine knowledge of, and where are their weaknesses? What do we need to know about what students have genuinely learned so that we can pay more attention to it and improve our instructional program? These are hard questions and ask for hard, critical self-evaluation by teachers.

The Barlow teachers have taken a hard look at their own work through the products they have received from their students. As a result, they identified areas of concern. Students were not writing creatively and not pushing the levels of their analytical work. Proofreading was weak and, in general, there is a sense that students did not push themselves to create high quality work — the standards were not being met to the level the teachers had hoped. The final "identified weakness" — "Students are paying attention to teachers' grades or content rather than quality of writing itself" — reveals the early stage of the process (despite years of work) this system is at. Breaking through the embedded culture of performing for a grade, and not achieving against a standard of quality, is a difficult norm to shift. This is a serious change in the unwritten rules of how school is presently played and students do not "get it" right away.

In the "Recommendations" list, the comment "Create a portfolio culture at JBHS" speaks directly to the writing-for-the-grade issue. The shift performance assessments ultimately demand is a cultural one in which the focus of classroom work and student work in general is measured against a standard of quality and is not a competitive quest for a letter or number grade. This is a difficult change to implement. Parents must be included in this conversation, so as to support the work of teachers in moving the school's culture from one of meaningless grading (What is an "A" worth, really?) to one which pursues quality work. The Joel Barlow staff has made a concerted effort to make such a move and has been willing to honestly self-reflect on their progress. The result is a constantly improving program of instruction and assessment where students and teachers are engaged together in active learning and self-improvement. It is a model which provides those interested in implementing performance assessments a path into unknown terrain — an exemplary reconnaissance mission for those willing to embark into the territory ahead.

STANDARDS, CRITERIA, AND RUBRICS

This chapter has provided teachers, students, parents, and administrators with ideas and examples to start a conversation about developing standards. Because students seldom know the expectations for the *quality* of their work, they proceed blindly through school, accepting subjective judgments about their progress. The provocation presented here asks that we open up the conversation about standards to the entire learning community, that teachers be given time to discuss this, and that administrators facilitate the progress of that conversation. This is a challenging task and, as the Joel Barlow example shows, it takes years to make progress. But consider the stakes: Can we afford to continue as we have, processing students through our classrooms, presenting them with material and tasks, and **not** providing clear feedback against known and valued standards? Is it fair to ask students to "achieve" *without* a clear enunciation of criteria and rubrics to work from?

Arguments can be made about the time and money which might be required to implement such a system of assessment, but those, ultimately, are arguments about priorities. If we do, indeed, care about the quality of student work, if we do, indeed, want our students to make continued *progress* toward standards of high quality, we can use our creativity and ingenuity to achieve those ends. Certainly it is a difficult and challenging task, and mistakes will be made along the way — but will those mistakes be any worse for our students than what they are subjected to now?

Clarifying standards, defining criteria, and developing rubrics is a worthy task for any number of reasons — the most important of which is the progress of our students. If we care about preparing our students for the 21st century, and if we believe performance assessments are an integral part of that preparation, there is little choice in the matter. To develop a performance assessment system *without* these deep and important conversations about standards, criteria, and rubrics would be to miss the point. The shift to new forms of assessment automatically means a shift in school culture, a changing of norms, the developing of new habits of instruction and evaluation. It is, on the face of it, an awesome task. It requires hard, ongoing work on the part of every member of a learning community. It means venturing into new territory, taking risks, changing our work and ourselves. But if the progress and success of our students is, in fact, our central concern, we have little choice in the matter.

We are at a significant point in our history. The standards debate gets to the heart of our visions of schooling in America. In many ways, the United States has become an emerging nation again, with scores of new immigrants, with the drive for inclusion and mainstreaming, with the Information Age upon us, we are faced with a set of challenges similar to those of the early 20th century. Despite our military and economic power, our educational system has stagnated; an outdated framework in a careening age. The greatest experiment in the Great Experiment of Democracy, the public school system, is faced with challenges its 19th century framework cannot meet. The factory system and Industrial Age have passed. The standards debate is one which is taking place in a new age, facing a new century. It demands that we begin the hard conversations about change which will lead to the transformation of our schools. The Great Experiment demands it and the school system requires it. It is incumbent upon us to accept the challenge.

5

PSYCHOMETRICIANS AT THE GATES!
ESTABLISHING VALIDITY THROUGH DOCUMENTATION: A WORKSHOP FOR CLASSROOM TEACHERS

Very few classroom teachers engage in discussions about *construct, criterion,* or *content* **validity** in faculty rooms or faculty meetings. The fact of the matter is, the issues of validity, reliability, generalizability, or comparability — in relation to testing or assessing — are virtually unknown to teachers. There may be a glimmer of recognition from a faculty member or two, based on some "research" or "statistics" course in their past. But the fact of the matter is, these concepts are the property of university researchers and commercial testmakers — two groups far removed from the day-to-day life of classrooms. And there's the rub! If we were asked to name what *drives* curriculum and instruction in the vast majority of public schools in this country, the answer is clear — state and national standardized tests. These one-shot, decontextualized events — more reliable than they are valid — are used to judge students, teachers, schools, and school systems.

The development of performance assessments, of course, has been a response to this mindless testing and this book has tried to document the progress being made along the way. But the testing industry (and make no mistake about the fact that this is *Big Business* we are talking about) casts a shadow which looms large over teachers, students, and schools. The discussion here is not "either/or;" rather, it is a call for perspective. What's the purpose for assessing our students? What do we hope to learn from the assessment? What do we hope they will learn from it? Does our test design insure we will get the information we need to answer those questions? Are these questions raised and examined by teachers, school boards, the community?

I raise those questions here because they are central to validity arguments. Schools (and, consequently, teachers and students) have become trapped within a testing system which, like the school structure itself, emerged in the first half of this century. It is based on a scientific empiricism which simplifies teaching and learning to a point of distortion. Students drill vocabulary words out-of-context to score higher on the SATs. Tutors are paid and cottage-industry companies pop-up like dandelions in the Spring to "prepare" people to **take** tests. What's taught, of course, are strategies and tactics — while your money-back guarantee insures *higher scores*! And is it any wonder, when we do a demographic study, that those students who live in the most affluent communities score highest on these exams?

My point is not to attack the testing industry, but to question their product — and to ask classroom teachers, administrators, and school boards to consider an approach to assessing students which might reframe the debate; a debate which invariably devolves into discussions about validity, reliability, generalizability, and comparability. But, given our relative ignorance about these topics, where are classroom teachers to begin?

The changing conceptions of validity generated by alternative, performance-based assessments have been articulately argued by

Lorrie A. Shepard (*Review of Educational Research*, 19 pp. 405–450), Pamela Moss (*Review of Educational Research*, Fall, 1992, pp. 229–258), Robert Linn, Eva Baker, and Stephen Dunbar (*Educational Researcher*, November, 1991, pp. 15–21), as well as Grant Wiggins (*Assessing Student Performance*, Chapter 7). Much of their work is based on the arguments of Messick, Cronbach, and Anastasi — all well-established members of the university research community. Little of this work ever reaches the desk of the average classroom teacher, however. As a result, teachers are susceptible to the pressures brought to bear by norm-referenced, standardized tests. These become the indicators of "success" or "failure" for too many teachers, students, and schools. But why?

Primarily because people, communities, *believe* in tests. They allow us to compare school districts and students because all the kids have been given the same questions for the same time period on the same day under similar conditions. Those are all the reasons these tests are *reliable*. But are they, in fact, valid? That is, do they really illustrate whether students have command or control of knowledge and skills? In fact, what we find is that test scores, in and of themselves, are meaningless. How they are *interpreted*, and by whom, is what gives them power. If the State Department of Education says a CAT, MEAP, Iowa, or other test is *important* — that the State will use the results to gauge the efficiency or effectiveness of a school — the test *interpretation* by the State gives the test power — particularly over curriculum and instruction. How test scores and test results are used, and by whom, is what gives tests weight. It does not necessarily make those tests valid.

As Pamela Moss points out, quoting Messick: " . . . [I]s the test any good as a measure of the characteristic it is interpreted to assess? . . . [S]hould the test be used for the proposed purpose?" Those questions, which have been raised again and again in the research community since the early '80s, get to the heart of the validity arguments. The first question is a simple one about *construct* validity: Does the test genuinely measure what it is supposed to be assessing? Most standardized tests, in fact, do not meet this criterion. Do students *genuinely* **know** vocabulary words if they are simply asked to select a synonym from four choices? Does matching analogies correctly mean a student can truly see patterns and think complexly about relationships? Maybe yes, maybe no. That our answer contains "may-be" calls the validity of these tests into question. More significantly, it raises the second question: Should these tests be used if they do not meet their intended purpose?

This is where a new argument about validity is being framed, an argument for *consequential validity*. That is, **what** is the test being used for? *How* is it being interpreted — and by whom — and to what end? Consequential validity raises the serious issues of ethical concern, which standardized tests, in their neatly homogenized, easily quantified "perfection," choose to ignore. It is on the edge of this new frontier of validity that performance assessments have pitched their tents. And it is up to those teachers and schools employing these assessments to send out the first scouting parties to see how consequential validity can be developed to establish these new "tests" as legitimate and significant.

WHERE DO WE BEGIN?

The most significant *consequence* of any assessment is its direct effect on teaching and learning. If our intent is for students to learn to use their minds well, we must ask them to perform "tests" in *contexts* which challenge them. Standardized testing does not do this; performance assessments do. Most standardized tests, as Wiggins notes (pp. 207–208), are simplistic stimulus-response designs. Performance assessments, on the other hand, are *contextualized, complex tasks* which ask students to **apply** knowledge and use intelligent judgment, providing evidence for their choices. Not only can they provide greater insight into student abilities, but they invariably contain a significant self-assessment component which aids the student in understanding his or her own progress. Most significant here, and that which most teachers clearly know, is that preparing students for any "high stakes" test determines the nature of classroom teaching and learning. A major *consequence* of testing, then, is the impact on classrooms — on curriculum and instruction.

This brings us back to where this book began. The old model of content-driven curriculum, delivered by direct teacher instruction, and audited by "objective" tests with truncated essays, is a system well-suited to standardized testing. The new model of curriculum and instruction which is embedded in complex, performance-based assessments, changes the very nature of teaching and learning. So, again, the *consequence* of the type of assessments we use is the direct impact it has on curriculum and instruction, teaching and learning. And this contributes to the genuine **validity** of performance assessments. This also raises serious challenges to those teachers and schools who commit to a performance assessment system.

Even though consequential validity can be convincingly argued to justify new assessments, I believe we need to address *construct* validity and *reliability*, too. It is important to focus on whether our performance assessments do, in fact, "measure" what they are intended to assess (construct validity). And, it is equally important to insure that our scoring is consistent and reliable — allowing for comparability and generalizability in some instances. So, where *do* we begin?

As has been stated again and again in this text, we begin with outcomes. What is it that we want students to know and be able to do? I would further qualify this question, though, by asking, "What *skills*, what *content*, and what *attitudes/dispositions* do we want our students to know and be able to exhibit or demonstrate?" While the question may seem relatively simple at first, this is one for which too many faculties come up with *simplistic* answers. Let me use a specific example, which provides a jumping-off point for designing a workshop to develop performance assessments featuring construct *and* consequential validity, which can be used reliably, and which provide some basis for comparability and generalizability.

WHERE'S THE BEEF? ESTABLISHING VALIDITY OF HIGHER-ORDER THINKING SKILLS

Most schools, when defining their outcomes, cite "critical thinking skills" as a desired trait in their graduates. This is a meaningless goal, unless we better define *what* it is we mean by "critical thinking skills" *and* then develop assessments for measuring those skills. And that's where performance assessments, and the schools attempting to implement them, often fall down. When asked, "**Which** *specific* critical thinking skills do you want your graduates to exhibit?," or, "Whose taxonomy of critical thinking skills are you using? (Bloom? Norris and Ennis? Richard Paul?)," people are invariably hard-pressed to answer because they haven't thought through what they mean by "critical thinking skills." Like "problemsolving" or producing "responsible citizens for a democratic society," these outcomes are vague and meaningless. Where's the **evidence** that our students are graduating with any of these outcomes?

These are important questions because they speak directly to the validity of our assessments. How are we measuring if our students are "critical thinkers," or "problemsolvers," or "responsible citizens?" What are the assessments we are using to test for these outcomes? And where's the documented evidence that our students have achieved them? Before we can become concerned with the *reliability* of our rubrics, criteria, and standards, before we can decide if our assessments are comparable or generalizable to others, we need to clearly establish valid measures which determine whether outcomes are being achieved by our students. But, before we can do that, we have to have a clear idea of what those outcomes are! To simply declare "critical thinking skills" is a desired outcome is not enough.

What I would like to present is a model workshop which any faculty or group of teachers could engage in to better define their outcomes. This, in turn, will contribute to the creation of more valid performance assessments — that is, assessments which will measure what they intend to assess (construct validity) **and** directly affect the teaching/learning process (consequential validity). Once teachers better understand this process, they can move into the realm of reliably scoring their assessments and then deciding on the generalizability or comparability of them.

WHERE'S THE BEEF? THE WORKSHOP

To establish what they mean by "critical thinking skills" teachers should be given several taxonomies of thinking skills. The best known of these, of course, is Bloom's taxonomy, in which *evaluation, synthesis,* and *analysis* are labeled "higher-order."

Another taxonomy which could be used is Robert Marzano's *Dimensions of Learning* construct. In it, Marzano divides thinking skills into four categories: (1) acquiring and integrating knowledge; (2) extending and refining knowledge; (3) using knowledge meaningfully; and (4) habits of mind. Marzano takes Bloom a step further by defining "critical thinking" into smaller, more clearly defined units. (Bloom's original work on cognitive processes, of course, goes to great lengths to do this; but, for most teachers, his taxonomy has been reduced to six categories — three "lower-order" and three "higher-order" thinking skills.) One taxonomy is not necessarily "better" than another. As with standardized test scores, it depends on how they are used or interpreted. What is necessary in conducting a workshop which engages teachers-as-learners and thinkers, is that they be presented with at least two taxonomies of critical thinking skills to consider.

Working individually at first, ask teachers to focus on which skills in either taxonomy they believe are truly *essential* for their students to graduate with. While we would want students to leave with the full complement of any taxonomy, the context of a workshop requires that participants focus on one or two *specific* critical thinking skills they deem essential. They should also be asked to consider *what it would look like* if students were engaged in using that critical thinking skill.

The workshop participants should then be broken into small groups (4–6 people) to compare their ideas and discuss *why* they chose the critical thinking skills they did. Groups should then be asked to decide on **three** critical skills they would like to focus on. *How* they decide on which skills to choose should be left for the groups to decide among themselves. (Note: The workshop, itself, becomes a critical thinking exercise for the participants.) Once they have decided on three, groups are asked to list their choices on newsprint and post them on a wall. Participants are then given time to "graze" the room, examining what other groups decided upon.

Reassembling in a large group, a short debriefing session should be held in which participants can ask questions of each other (regarding their choices or any other "burning issues" which arise), as well as the *process* of *how* groups made decisions. After informing participants that they will return to these critical thinking skills, the second phase of the workshop is introduced — an exercise I like to call "Unpacking Sizer."

UNPACKING EXHIBITIONS: EXAMINING CRITICAL THINKING SKILLS

Presented with two different Exhibitions from Theodore Sizer's *Horace's School* (Fig. 5.1), workshop participants must "unpack"

FIGURE 5.1: EXHIBITION: KNOWLEDGE IN USE

Science:

Act as the school's nutritionist: the cafeteria has $2.56 to spend per full single serving for lunch. Design three menus, each of which is

1) within that budget allowance
2) maximally nutritious, and
3) maximally attractive to students in your school.

You will have to consult the various tables and data displayed in the current nutritionist's guide available in the library and the cafeteria office. Be prepared to defend your definition of "nutritious" and "attractive" and your particular menus. You will submit your entries to an all-school poll, and the winning six menus will be served during the next term.

Mathematics:

1. A recent study reported that of the two million cancer deaths in this country each year, three hundred are related directly to an improper diet. The study went on to state that the overall life expectancy of cancer victims would have increased by three months if all victims had followed a proper diet. Several of your classmates argue that three months isn't much to gain for sacrificing some favorite foods for the rest of one's life. Explain how the report has seriously misled your classmates. Provide mathematical evidence rather than philosophical reasoning as the basis for your explanation.

2.   A. Describe how you would measure the distance between your ears without using calipers.

   B. When you are satisfied with the methods you have devised, compare the result with that obtained by using calipers. Discuss what you need to do to make you methods almost as reliable as using calipers.

   C. Carry out your plan and describe the result.

   D. Critique your work.

From *Horace's School,* pp. 98–100

these complex problems to determine which critical thinking skills students would have to use to succeed in each task. The challenges for the workshop participants are:

♦ List the *specific* critical thinking skills students would have to demonstrate in "solving" each Exhibition.

♦ Describe what students would *look like* as they demonstrated use of critical thinking skills in each Exhibition.

♦ Describe what activities, performance assessments, mini-exhibitions, etc., students would have to have engaged in *prior to* being presented with these Exhibition tasks.

Give participants a sizable block of time to complete these exercises. It is highly important that people talk about an exercise like this *as they are doing it*. Analyzing the Exhibitions for their specific critical thinking skills, participants will begin to understand how they can develop their own Exhibitions based on "critical thinking skills."

Facilitating discussions which directs people to answer the guiding questions, begins to reveal how Exhibitions and planning backwards from them, when clear outcomes are defined, can lead to thorough and valid assessments. By using Sizer's Exhibitions, participants can tease out the critical thinking skills students would have to employ to genuinely accomplish the tasks at hand. By thinking through how students would have to prepare for these Exhibitions, curriculum and instruction reveal themselves! What begins to unfurl is the key to the process of developing valid performance assessments.

Questions which help facilitate the debriefing of this exercise are these:

♦ What critical thinking skills can we identify in Sizer's Exhibitions? (Go through each Exhibition, eliciting responses.)

♦ In what ways does this "unpacking" exercise help clarify how we can more clearly define critical thinking skills?

♦ Describe what it would look like when students were engaged in preparing for and presenting these Exhibitions? What do you see them doing?

♦ Describe what students would have to do *prior to* these Exhibitions to be properly prepared to execute them. Explain how those descriptions begin to inform your conception of curriculum and instruction design. Discuss the implications of this. Would content have to be "cut out?" If so, what? How would this change teacher/student interactions in the classroom? What materials and resources would students and teachers need to accomplish these tasks and any of the work leading up to the assignment of these tasks.

♦ How would you **document** student work as evidence that they have really acquired the critical thinking skills we have identified as outcomes? How can we insure that our **documentation** would be *substantial evidence* of student achievement?

These last questions are most important, and we will return to them after we look at two other exercises which will push the thinking, and the work, of workshop participants.

UNPACKING STANDARDIZED TESTS; UNPACKING OURSELVES; GUT CHECK!

Using the same process we applied to Sizer's Exhibitions, ask participants to consider the following: What would you discover if you "unpacked" a standardized test? What critical thinking skills — based on the taxonomies of thinking skills — would be revealed by standardized tests? Would student performance on those tests *genuinely* reflect knowledge and control of critical thinking skills? It is a true challenge for anyone to think of any kind of multiple choice questions which genuinely reveal higher-order thinking skills. This is not to say that there aren't any out there — and certainly people at ETS are working to develop more rigorous exams which do test these abilities. But, the fact of the matter is, the format and context of standardized tests, or even classroom-teacher developed multiple-choice or matching-item tests, are not designed to probe deep and critical thought.

Ask participants to take an assessment they use, or any assessment used at their school, and "unpack" it in the same way. What begins to happen, once people become involved in the process of looking to see what *outcomes* an assessment reveals, is that the shallowness of most tests — whether school, state, or nationally developed — becomes glaringly apparent. With that in mind, ask participants to return to the critical thinking skills they identified in their small groups in the first exercise of the workshop.

Based on those critical thinking skills, ask participants to develop a complex, contextualized Exhibition which would require students to demonstrate they could employ (and explain the employment of) those critical thinking skills. This, of course, is no easy task — particularly if people are not in the habit of developing Exhibitions based on clearly defined outcomes. But this is a crucial point in the workshop, because it pushes the participants to actually take the theory of planning backwards, combined with their (new?) analysis of critical thinking skills, and synthesize their knowledge in a tangible product. While asking for active involvement, participants are given the opportunity to create a curriculum and instruction *product* which reflects their understanding of a *process* of curriculum and assessment development. Again, the beauty of this workshop is that is embodies the kind of critical thinking Exhibition it hopes to create for students!

Not content to merely help workshop participants develop a useful assessment tool for their schools, we need to push people to consider how they will document student work in ways that clearly prove its validity. Beyond *what* students will do to exhibit their critical thinking skills, then, teachers and administrators need to seriously think through how they will **record the evidence of student achievement.** With that, assessment designers must be prepared to present and defend their plan for assessment implementation and documentation which will satisfy any questions about validity.

Rather than discussing the possibilities for documentation at this point (workshop participants need to be allowed to exercise their own thoughts and creativity, unsullied by a facilitators point of view), let's consider an exercise which can help people critically examine their work, offering constructive feedback for improvement. We will return to the possibilities for documentation after examining a process, created by Joe McDonald at the Coalition of Essential Schools, referred to as "The Tuning Protocol."

The Tuning Protocol establishes a systematic process for any group working on assessments to present their work, receive honest feedback on it, and consider how to best implement what they have developed. Because getting (and giving) feedback can be a difficult and sensitive process, the Tuning Protocol was designed to establish parameters which facilitate a "safe" environment for presenters and critics.

First proposed in Joe McDonald's *Three Pictures of an Exhibition* (part of the Coalition of Essentials Schools "Studies on Exhibitions" series), the model presented here is a variation of the original. As with all work in performance assessments, designers should always see the *process* piece as adaptable, suiting it to their needs and ends. In this case, we would ask people to use the categories McDonald recommends for giving feedback: *warm, cool,* and *hard.* The process by which that feedback is given is presented here in the context of our "Where's the Beef?" workshop — it can serve as a model or template for any setting where assessment or curriculum designers desire feedback to their work. (For a view of the "Tuning Protocol" in another setting, *see* McDonald, *Graduation by Exhibition,* ASCD publication, pp. 48–54.)

The categories ask for a series of responses from several perspectives. A *warm* response identifies what we see as positive in the work and comes from a "friendly" perspective. The *cool* response is more objective, probing more deeply with questions, trying to analyze the substance of the work being examined. The *hard* response looks to align the work with standards of validity, reliability, and equity; that is, Does the assessment measure what we want it to (is it valid)? Do we agree about standards and criteria which will be used (is it reliable)? Are the outcomes clearly known so that standards of achievement can be accomplished in a reasonable fashion (matters of equity)? In all cases, the feedback is offered from the perspective of a "critical friend." The objective is *not* to tear the work to ribbons, but to work collegially, producing an assessment which best serves students and continually improves our curriculum.

The *warm, cool,* and *hard* feedback is delivered in a structured fashion, to insure assessments are presented as clearly as possible, and to guarantee that feedback is heard. In an ideal setting, a long block of time is set aside for the "tuning protocol" process. While it can be done in 15–30 minutes, it is recommended that participants be given *at least* an hour. The "tuning" process is broken into three distinct time blocks, each with *very specific* procedures for the participants. (Note: Time can be divided into segments of 5–10 minutes; 10–15 minutes; 15–20 minutes, or more, if desired. The only "rule" is that all Blocks be given equal amounts of time.)

FIRST BLOCK

Assessment designers present their work. Clear explanation should be given as to which outcomes the assessment is intended to address. Expectations of students work — what it will "look" like, how it will be evaluated, tasks students will perform, etc. — should be presented. A clear explanation of how student work will be documented should be part of this presentation. The *Feedback Group* will take notes, listening carefully, but *will not* interrupt this presentation for questions or comments. This procedure is very important — it allows the presenters to explain their entire design while forcing the listeners to focus on what is being presented, noting their questions, comments, etc., in *writing*. The presenting group can be given these notes after the Protocol is finished, thereby having documentary reminders about the process.

SECOND BLOCK

The *Feedback Group* gives *warm, cool,* and *hard* feedback, based on their listening notes. The *Feedback Group* should work out their own process for presenting comments — that is, who goes when, etc. The feedback should be presented in the *warm, cool, hard* order. During this block, the Presenters *only listen,* taking notes on what they hear. This should not deteriorate into a question and answer session (a rule which should be strictly enforced).

THIRD BLOCK — THE CONVERSATION

The presenting group initiates conversation by responding to some of the questions and/or comments from the *Feedback Group*. Based on the Presenters response, the *Feedback Group* now engages in the give-and-take conversation about assessment design, standards, and documentation, always looking to clarify and help improve the work of the Presenters. The groups then reverse roles to do the protocol a second time.

POST-THIRD BLOCK

Once everyone has participated in the Tuning Protocol, all parties should be brought back together for a debriefing about what was learned. The Protocol, as a process, should also be assessed, with people commenting on "what worked" and "what didn't" in their groups. In this way, the Tuning Protocol and its subsequent debriefing become a minimodel of the assessment design, as well as a troubleshooting process. Beyond this, we should also consider what our "next steps" are going to be in pushing our work with performance assessments further. With careful planning, employing a thoughtful, methodical process, we can consistently improve the quality of student work, curriculum, instruction, and assessment.

DOCUMENTATION: TRIANGULATION AND BEYOND

One Achilles Heel of the school reform movement, up to this point in time, has been the documentation of compelling evidence which supports the effectiveness of performance assessments. As the previous chapters clearly testify, performance assessments are alive and well all over the country. Students are engaged in authentic tasks and producing quality work at numerous schools. Yet, there is a lingering, haunting criticism — prove these work *better* than the testing system which exists. And the critics have a right to make their charge. Those of us engaged in implementing new assessments *need to* present a stronger case for what we are doing. Too often, the reaction to these charges is a defensive one: *What do you mean? Come in and look at what our kids are doing!* And, indeed, students are *performing* and *producing*. The presentation of *what* the students are doing and producing, **in relation to clearly stated outcomes**, however, is often lacking.

Because we are so excited about what we see our students doing, because we know on intuitive and cognitive levels the quality of their work is improving, we cannot understand why people simply won't *believe* us. One problem is that our reaction to our students' work is a *warm* one. We know these kids; we've worked with them; we're invested in them — and we *do* know how much progress they've made. Nonetheless, "take my word for it, these kids are doing quality work," is a difficult argument to make against the monolithic statistics of ETS, the New York State Regents, or even against some teacher's meticulously detailed grade book which accounts for attendance, homework, tests, quizzes, and essays. America loves a good, quick quantification: "What's the bottom line?" "Show me the figures on that." "Give it to me on one page."

But America also loves *evidence*. *Perry Mason, L.A. Law, Law and Order,* the O.J. Simpson trial — we are nation that wants to see proof — we love the drama of the courtroom. And performance assessments, in their infancy, have not provided enough substantial evidence to drive the bean-counters from the schools. We need to take the case to the court of public opinion with our briefcases packed with evidence! What I propose here is a systematic approach to **documenting** the work we do with performance assessments so that there will be *no doubt* left in anyone's mind as to how effective these instruments are.

Borrowing from the increasingly popular *qualitative* research community, I believe careful documentation built around the concept of *triangulation* can serve to establish the *construct* validity of performance assessments. The *consequential* validity of these instruments is a relatively easy case to make — but by documenting our work more meticulously we can also buttress those claims. Most important to note here, as was emphasized in the "Where's the Beef?" workshop, is that documentation of assessments **must** become part of the design, right from the start. Planning *is not complete* without a documentation component. The documentation must directly address a clearly stated outcome. And, in many cases, **one** piece of evidence is not enough. Hence, the need for triangulation.

Simply put, triangulation means collecting evidence from three (and sometimes more) sources which will substantiate whatever claim you are making. In this case, our "claim" is the outcome(s) students are to demonstrate. How have we documented this? Most often, we have a *record* of the student work — and sometimes the work itself, as an artifact. When trying to convince a public which believes in psychometrics, however, this may not be seen as substantial, compelling evidence. We need, therefore, to insure that we have documented student achievement in a variety of forms which speak to our outcomes and make our case compelling — beyond a reasonable doubt.

How can we implement a systematic, triangulated approach to collecting evidence of student exhibition of desired outcomes?

Because of the constraints of time, resources, materials, etc., we may not be able to do it *every time* we use a performance assessment. But we should be able to institutionalize certain methods of evidence collection which will *always* contribute to making our case for student achievement. For example, we can always start with the ***product*** of student work — whether it's a piece of writing, a poster, the detailed written solution to a problem, a lab report, and so on. We can obviously examine that artifact to see if it directly reflects achievement of a stated outcome. Does the essay illustrate probing analysis? Are the steps described in the problemsolving process sensible and effective? Does the artwork reflect of synthesis of ideas studied over the last month?

Next, we should consider having students write a short, reflective piece, which directly addresses (through a prompt) the outcome sought and the student's understanding of it. For example, for some critical thinking skills we might use the following prompt(s):

- ♦ Please describe the steps of your thinking process as you
  - (composed your essay about *Hamlet*.)
  - (began to design your lab to solve the photosynthesis problem.)
  - (decided how to answer the dog-pen/area-perimeter problem.)

A student's response to a prompt like this will not only provide a "window" into the student's thinking but will also give us another evidentiary artifact to make our case with.

A teacher's observation log or checksheet (which provides for anecdotal comments) can also serve as more support for student progress or achievement. A carefully documented account of what most teachers now do every day — but quite ***informally*** — would provide a wonderful counterpoint document to the student's reflective piece. In the process, we will have accumulated more evidence about *student performance.*

The use of audio- and/or videotape, of course, is clearly a documentary record of student work which "saves the moment" while providing irrefutable evidence of *what* students did *when,* and *how well* they did whatever the work was at the time. Audio recordings of interviews, conferences, reflections, conversations, debriefings, and so on, can be a compelling account of student work. Sometimes photographs can serve to show the what, where, how, and how well, of student achievement. Once teachers begin to consider *documentation* as an integral and important aspect of performance assessment design, there are many, many possibilities which exist — or can be created — for accumulating evidence about student progress. The crucial point here is that performance assessment designers need to see *documentation* as the logical meeting point of a circle which starts with "stated outcomes."

FIGURE 5.2: DOCUMENTATION

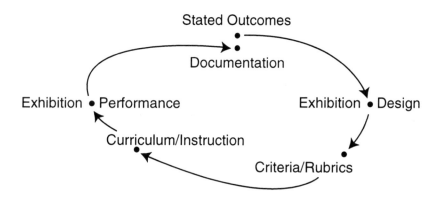

THE TIME! THE PAPERWORK! WHERE DO WE STORE ALL THIS? . . . AND "WHAT IF?"

Performance assessments take more time than "objective" tests. We know that. There is far more paperwork, videotapes, audiotapes, artwork, posters, charts, maps, graphs, lab reports, etc., than most teachers presently handle. We know that, too. And now I'm proposing we triangulate our evidence to substantiate that these assessments truly achieve what we claim they do. How can we do it?

Let me digress for a moment. There is a simple puzzle which presents the perfect metaphor for what we're talking about. While many people are familiar with this puzzle, I'll run the risk of presenting it here to make my point.

Connect all 9 dots with 4 straight lines *without* taking your pen/pencil off the page.

The solution, of course, is that you have to go *outside the box* (see the solution on next page). There is no instruction saying the four lines have to conform with the rectangle — that is a stricture which is self-imposed based on an internal construct. We see nine dots arranged in three rows of threes and we assume that they *must be* connected within the bounds of the rectangle they *seem* to outline.

My contention is that the structure of schools and schooling are those nine dots. Because most of us have attended the public schools and then have gone on to teach in those same schools, we think that there is a structure which *must* exist, immutable and unchangeable. And, because of that, because of years of living and working within that structure, we believe that everything *must* operate in a certain way. We have lost the perspective to consider getting **outside the box** and imagining other ways of "doing school."

Performance assessments are a different way to "do" school. But if we are to use them effectively, we are going to discover that they push up against other structures and ideas which exist within the box, within the nine unconnected dots. The schedule. Report cards. Testing. Curriculum and instruction. If we are going to implement performance assessments the way they are described in this book — and if we are going to document those assessments as detailed here — then we are going to have to get *outside the box*.

The Solution

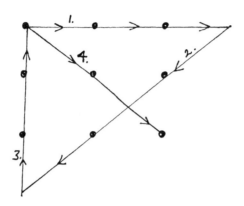

- Does every student have to be given the same assessment on the same day? (Why?) Couldn't we assess five on Monday, five on Tuesday, five on Wednesday, etc? (That is, have them "turn work in" or perform on those days — and not have to collect (or watch?) 25 on FRIDAY and have the *Weekend from Hell!*)
- Could report cards be issued in the course of a 3-week span, rather than on the same day? And could they actually contain useful feedback information for parents and students (and next year's teacher!)?
- *What if* teams of teachers were responsible for a **total** cohort of students (that is, 5 teachers responsible for 125 students) for the whole day, arranging the schedule (and the assessment schedule) as they see fit?
- *What if* students were made more responsible for self-assessment, peer-assessment, group and class assessment?
- *What if* students were made responsible for keeping track of their own documentation — because without it they cannot advance or graduate!
- *What if* we are able to obtain the technology to transfer paperwork, and video, and audio, into digitized records of student performance? (*Surprise!* There are already

schools engaged in the first phases of this. Personal computers, CD-ROMs, scanners, software programs, etc., are already available or on the way.)

♦   *What if* we began to genuinely integrate curriculum, designed around inquiry-based, problemsolving, question-driven work? How might that change *everything* we do?

♦   *What if* we looked at longer school days in which guaranteed teacher-to-teacher professional time was built into the schedule for daily curriculum, instruction, and assessment planning and designing? And the same for longer school years (that is, don't extend student days, but build in additional days for teachers to work together on curriculum and instruction)?

♦   *What if* teachers (and the teacher unions), administrators, school boards, parents, and community organizations began to work as *partners* rather than *adversaries*?

Sounds impossible? Only if you stay inside the box. Change won't happen quickly, but that doesn't mean it *can't* happen. It has taken 100 years to put the present system solidly in place. Schools are not going to change radically or move quickly in any new direction. But that does not mean it *can't* happen. Careful thought and planning, a willingness to take risks, and a commitment to the belief that changes need to occur to save the children of this country are the first steps outside the box and into the Territory Ahead.

There are already some pioneers out there — this book is full of them. You don't have to make the journey alone. And you don't have to complete it by nightfall — or even by next September. You only have to take that first step. Go ahead. You may find that getting outside the box and into the Territory Ahead is an interesting and exciting place to be; one where students *want to* come to school and where quality achievement is the norm; where schools are thriving learning communities and intellectual stimulation and exciting ideas are the norm. Idealistic? Naive? Or simply a different vision? A vision from outside the box. A vision from the Territory Ahead.

Go ahead. Take a step.

BIBLIOGRAPHY

Adler, Mortimer J. (1982) *The Paideia Proposal,* Macmillan Publishing, New York, NY

Adler, Mortimer J. (1983) *Paideia Problems and Possibilities,* Macmillan Publishing, New York, NY

Adler, Mortimer J. (1984) *The Paideia Program,* Macmillan Publishing, New York, NY

Angelo, T. & Cross, K.P. (1993) *Classroom Assessment Techniques,* Jossey-Bass Publishers, San Francisco, CA

Archbald, D. & Newman, F. (1988) *Beyond Standardized Testing: Authentic Academic Achievement in the Secondary School.* Reston, VA: NASSP Publications

Belanoff, P. & Dickson, M. (eds.) (1991) *Portfolios: Process and Product,* Boynton/Cook Publishers, Heinemann, Portsmouth, NH

Berlak, Harold, et al (1992) *Toward a New Science of Educational Testing and Assessment,* NY: State University of New York Press

Board of Education, City of Chicago. (1991) *Introducing the Socratic Seminar into the Secondary School Classroom,* Bd. of Ed. City of Chicago, IL

Brandt, Ronald (ed.) (1992) *Performance Assessment,* ASCD, Alexandria, VA

Burke, Kay (ed.) (1992) *Authentic Assessment: A Collection*, IRI/Skylight Publishing, Palatine, IL

Burke, Kay (1993) *The Mindful School: How to Assess Thoughtful Outcomes*, IRI/Skylight Publishing, Palatine, IL

Edgerton, R., Hutchings, P., & Quinlan, K. (1991) *The Teaching Portfolio*, American Association for Higher Education, Washington, DC

Fairtest, (1990) *Standardized Tests and Out Children: A Guide to Testing Reform*, The National Center for Fair & Open Testing, Cambridge, MA

Fullan, M. (with Stiegelbauer, S.), (1991) *The New Meaning of Educational Change*, Teachers College Press, New York, NY

Gardner, H. (1985) *Frames of Mind*, Basic Books, Inc. Publishers, New York, NY

Graves, D. & Sunstein, B. (eds.) (1992) *Portfolio Portraits*, Heinemann, Portsmouth, NH

Hargreaves, Andy, (1989) *Curriculum and Assessment Reform*, Open University Press, Philadelphia, PA

Harvard Educational Review, (Spring, 1994) *Symposium: Equity in Educational Assessment*, Cambridge, MA

Herman, J., Aschbacher, P. & Winters, L. (1992) *A Practical Guide to Alternative Assessment*, ASCD, Alexandria, VA

Johnson, B. (Winter, 1992) "Creating Performance Assessments" *Holistic Education Review*, Brandon, VT

Kulm, G. (ed.) (1990) *Assessing Higher Order Thinking in Mathematics*, American Association for the Advancement of Science, Washington, DC

Kulm, G. (1994) *Mathematics Assessment: What Works in the Classroom* Jossey-Bass, San Francisco, CA

Linn, R., Baker, E., & Dunbar, S. (1991) "Complex, Performance-Based Assessment: Expectations and Validation Criteria," *Educational Researcher*, 20, 8 pp. 15–21 (November)

Maeroff, G. (1991) "Assessing Alternative Assessment," *Phi Delta Kappan*, 73, 4; pp. 272–281 (December)

Marzano, R., Pickering, D., & McTighe, J. (1993) *Assessing Student Outcomes*, Association of Supervision & Curriculum Development, Alexandria, VA

McDonald, J. et al. (1993) *Graduation by Exhibition*, ASCD, Alexandria, VA

Mitchell, Ruth (1992) *Testing for Learning*, Free Press/Macmillan, New York, NY

Murphy, S. & Smith, M. (1991) *Writing Portfolios*, Pippin Publishing Ltd., Ontario, Canada

Neill, M. et al. (1995) *Implementing Performance Assessments*, Fairtest: The National Center for Fair & Open Testing, Cambridge, MA

Perrone, V. (ed.) (1991) *Expanding Student Assessment for Supervision and Curriculum*, ASCD, Alexandria, VA

Potter, J. (ed.) (1991) *Conversations about Assessment*, College of Education, University of Southern Maine, Gorham, ME

Rowntree, D. (1977) *Assessing Students: How Shall We Know Them?*, Nichols Publishing Co., New York, NY

Sarason, S. (1990) *The Predictable Failure of Educational Reform*, Jossey-Bass Publishers, San Francisco, CA

Selden, P. (1991) *The Teaching Portfolio*, Anker Publishing Co., Bolton, MA

Shepard, L. (1989) "Why We Need Better Assessments," *Educational Leadership*, 46, 7, pp. 4–7 (April)

Sizer, T. (1992) *Horace's School*, Houghton Mifflin, Boston, MA

Stiggins, R., Rubel, E., & Quellmalz, E. (1988) *Measuring Thinking Skills in the Classroom*, NEA Publication, Washington, DC

Stiggins, R. (1991) "Assessment Literacy," *Phi Delta Kappan*, 72, 1 pp. 534–539 (March)

Stiggins, R. (1994) *Student-Centered Classroom Assessment*, Merrill/Macmillan Publishers, New York, NY

Tierney, R., Carter, M. & Desai, L. (1991) *Portfolio Assessment in the Reading-Writing Classroom*, Christopher-Gordon Publishers, Norwood, MA

U.S. Congress, Office of Technology Assessment. *Testing in American Schools: Asking the Right Questions*, OTA–SET–519, US Government Printing Office, Washington, DC (February, 1992)

U.S. Department of Labor. (1991) *What Work Requires of Schools: A SCANS (Secretary's Commission on Achieving Necessary Skills) Report for America 2000,* US Government Printing Office, Washington, DC

Vermont Department of Education. (1989) *Vermont Writing Assessment: The Portfolio,* State of Vermont, Dept. of Education

Wiggins, G. (1993) *Student Performance: Exploring the Purpose and Limits of Testing,* Jossey-Bass, San Francisco, CA

Wiggins, G. (1991) *Toward One System of Education: Assessing to Improve,Not Merely Audit,* Education Commission of the States, Denver, CO

Wiggins, G. (1988) "Rational Numbers: Scoring and Grading that Helps Rather Than Hurts Learning," *American Educator* pp. 20–48 (Winter)

Wiggins, G. (1989) "A True Test: Toward More Authentic and Equitable Assessment," *Phi Delta Kappan.* 70, 9: 703–713 (May)

Wiggins, G. (1989) "Teaching to the (Authentic) Test," *Educational Leadership,* 46, 7, pp. 41–47 (April)

Wiggins, G. (1991) "Standards, Not Standardization: Evoking Quality Student Work," *Educational Leadership* 48, 5, pp. 18–25 (February)

Wiggins, G. (1992) "Creating Tests Worth Taking" *Educational Leadership* 49, 8, pp. 26–33 (May)

Wiggins, G. (1994) "None of the Above," *The Executive Educator,* 16, 7, pp. 14–18

Wolf, D., Bixby, J., Glen III, J., & Gardner, H. (1991) "To Use their Minds Well: Investigating New Forms of Student Assessment," in Grant, G. (ed.) (1991) *Review of Research in Education,* Washington, DC, American Educational Research Association, pp. 31–74

Wolf, D. (1987/88) "Opening Up Assessment," *Educational Leadership* 44, 4 (December/January)

Wolf, D. (1989) "Portfolio Assessment: Sampling Student Work," *Educational Leadership* 46, 7, pp. 35–39 (April)